"An Extraordinary Book from a Super Extraordinary Human Being."
> —**Cathy Hughes, Founder and Chairperson,**
> **TV One/Radio One, INC.**

"Pickard's career as an entrepreneur and businessman is a true American story of success achieved through perseverance, determination, and a keen mind. His successes as a businessman and entrepreneur are matched by his passion and commitment to serve his community and to mentor young people. His book is a must read for anyone who wishes to learn the lesson of how to do well while also doing good."
> —*Marc H. Morial, President and CEO, National Urban League*

"Dr. Bill Pickard's thought-provoking wisdom helped shift my corporate mindset to entrepreneurship during our first encounter. Now, more than 25 years later, his prolific business advice, life lessons and mentorship continue to be invaluable. Anyone in pursuit of the unconventional and determined to be successful despite failures, should read Dr. Pickard's book *Millionaire Moves*."
> —**Hiram E. Jackson, Chief Executive Officer, Real Times Media**

"This book is something we have all been waiting for....when you have a dedicated entrepreneur like Dr. Pickard who has always been willing to share not just his financial blessings but his wisdom, his positive attitude, his relationships and his faith..... you have everything that you need to be a success not just in business but also in life. I can bear witness that he a is man in love with his people and their achievement."
> —**Harry E. Johnson, Sr.,**
> **President, Martin Luther King National Memorial**
> **and Former President of Alpha Phi Alpha Fraternity**

"As a respected and successful entrepreneur, Dr. Pickard's publication, *Seven Proven Principles of Entrepreneurship*, will ensure future generations have a guidepost to exceptional business achievement. Dr. Pickard has proven that entrepreneurship and philanthropy can serve as mutual partners for the positive benefit of society. I am honored that Saint Augustine's University Business School will have this publication as an anchor for our entrepreneurship program."
> —**Dr. Everett B. Ward, President, Saint Augustine's University**

"William Pickard, former co-director of the Urban Entrepreneurship program at University of Michigan's Institute of Labor and Industrial Relations, has distilled his years of experience creating a range of businesses into keys to entrepreneurial success. While targeted to individuals, his insights also have important implications for community development—in his own words, creating the economic resources needed 'to make a neighborhood hum…'"

—Lawrence S. Root, Professor,
School of Social Work, University of Michigan

"An insightful, motivating, illuminating and instructional guide to entrepreneurship, a must read if you ever want to achieve success in today's business environment. Having personally witnessed Dr. Pickard's triumphs in business and been counseled first hand by his wisdom, I am confident that the insights in *Millionaire Moves* can help hard working entrepreneurs become prosperous business owners."

—Toni Rodgers, McDonald's Franchise Owner and Entrepreneur

"Dr. Pickard's honest and provocative insight offers a blueprint to entrepreneurship for millennials to follow that's authentic and relatable to my generation."

—Peter Bailey,
Author & NiteCap Media Founder

"*Millionaire Moves: Seven Proven Principles of Entrepreneurship* is a must read for those serious about growing their businesses. As more African Americans are entering the entrepreneurial space, this book is timely and on point. Dr. Pickard's seven principles are simplistic yet profound. Congratulations, Dr. Pickard!"

—Ron Busby, Sr.
President and CEO U.S. Black Chambers, Inc.

"This book is entertaining and full of metaphors and engaging stories that provide a window into Dr. Pickard's world of proven and practical insights, methods and tools. As the past dean of a college of business, I have seen first-hand how his pragmatic approach to business ownership adds value to classroom discussions and provides immediately actionable advice to seasoned entrepreneurs."

—Dr. Le-Quita Booth,
former Dean of Alabama State University School of Business

"I have used Dr. William Pickard's transferable entrepreneurial insights to run one of the most successful fraternal organizations in the USA."

—**Melvin Bazemore, Esq.**
Lt Grand Commander & COO, United Supreme Council,
Ancient Accepted Scottish Rite (PHA)

"*Millionaire Moves: Seven Proven Principles of Entrepreneurship* is a life-changing, inspiring, and thought-provoking masterpiece that is a profoundly insightful and electrifying 'must read' for all entrepreneurs and aspiring entrepreneurs who aspire to reach the pinnacle of business success."

—**Dr. Millicent Lownes-Jackson,**
Dean, The College of Business, Tennessee State University

"Bill Pickard is a self-made entrepreneur who has not only survived in business but has thrived over 40 years. The principles that he outlines in his book, *Millionaire Moves: Seven Proven Principles of Entrepreneurship,* can serve as a Blueprint for young entrepreneurs around the world."

—**Lecester (Bill) Allen,**
Founder and President of the Allen Entrepreneurial
Institute International (AEII) at Camp Exposure

"*Millionaire Moves: Seven Proven Principles of Entrepreneurship* by Dr. William F. Pickard is a delightful overview on the way we do business in the twenty-first century. He writes with humor that cleverly and explosively makes you laugh, cry, feel encouraged, probably even get mad and, most importantly, think. Read this book at the risk of causing a positive change in your life or business. A must read for all entrepreneurs or those inspiring to be an entrepreneur."

—**Anthony Negbenebor, Ph.D., Dean Emeritus and Dover Chair of**
Business, Gardner-Webb University, Past President, Accreditation
Council for Business Schools and Programs (ACBSP)

"*Millionaire Moves* is a fascinating confirmation that for every remarkable entrepreneur there is an equally remarkable story. Dr. Pickard's real-life experiences are a colorful backdrop for seven core principles that aspiring and seasoned entrepreneurs should consider gospel. This book sharpens the ground game of today's entrepreneur with it's practical, real-world approach."

—**Cory Ackerman,**
Founder LeRoi Products –
"Staci Maxwell" brand of home and gift products

"Dr. Pickard's *Seven Proven Principles* is a testimony of the years of experience from a very successful entrepreneur. As an academic in the business world, I can fully appreciate the steps relevant to what we might teach in the typical business curriculum. I think the value-add of Dr. Pickard's prescription, however, is found in the steps 'Relationships,' 'Failure,' and 'Faith.' While generally not covered in the academic discussion of successful entrepreneurial skills, these steps are vital to long-term entrepreneurial success. His book discloses the whole story, not just the shiny side."

Alicia Jackson, Dean,
College of Business, Albany State University

"This is an excellent book. Dr. Pickard is a highly successful entrepreneur who has always been willing to share his knowledge, wisdom, and life experience with folks who aspire to be successful. Reading this book provides you with all you need to achieve success in both business and life endeavors."

—Mo Sarhan, Dean and Professor,
College of Business Administration, Savannah State University.

"This book absolutely captures the essence of one of our most distinguished black business leaders, and does it in a way that is highly instructive for both aspiring and experienced entrepreneurs alike. Not only is Dr. Pickard's personal journey inspiring, he gives his readers the gift of a proven roadmap that reveals the optimal path to success in any operating environment."

—Sonya S. Mays,
President and CEO, Develop Detroit

"Dr. Pickard uses his talent and generosity to significantly impact the lives of those who cross his path. As he outlines his seven principles of successful entrepreneurship, you can imagine his voice coming through the pages. His life's work demonstrates each principle and, as a man of faith, he also demonstrates his sincere desire to pour into others what he has learned along the way. I see this book as a gift to us all."

—Wanda F. Lester, Ph.D.
Interim Dean, School of Business,
North Carolina Central University

"Dr. Pickard shared his seven principles of entrepreneurship when I was a very young man. Looking back some 30 plus years, I can now see how they have changed my life—helping me to transform from a child of a single mom with a welfare background into the leader of Global Operations for the world's largest hotel company. I met Dr. Pickard when he spearheaded a scholarship and mentoring program that took high school minority students from Detroit and Flint and gave them a formal college education focused on business. In addition to our classroom studies, he personally spent time teaching us how to succeed in business whether working for someone or working for yourself. His lessons have been incredibly valuable to me and countless other professionals. If you want the keys to being a successful entrepreneur, I strongly encourage you to read this book!"

—**Ray Bennett,**
Chief Global Officer, Global Operations,
Marriott International, GVSU, Class of 1991

"Dr. Pickard shares the principles that propelled his meteoric success in a very pragmatic, understandable, and actionable way. His personal example of taking a holistic approach to business success is appropriately steeped in personal commitment, growth, intentionality, hard work and faith. *Millionaire Moves* is a must-read primer, guide and resource not only for business success, but for success in life!"

—**Jerome Hutchinson, Jr.**
Founder & Chief Servant Officer,
ICABA-International Career and Business Alliance, Inc.

"Dr. Pickard's engaging and illuminating narrative speaks to the best in us all. I think his seven principles are essential fertilizer for young minds seeking to overcome fear and negativity. Blessed with the ability to deftly navigate class and culture Pickard draws the reader in with both empathy and inspiration. As an artist and educator in Harlem NYC, I see the immense worth of voices like Dr. Pickard's as the next generation ripens."

—**M. Scott Johnson,**
Internationally renowned sculptor and educator at the
Schomburg Center for Research in Black Culture

MILLIONAIRE MOVES

SEVEN PROVEN PRINCIPLES OF ENTREPRENEURSHIP

MILLIONAIRE MOVES

SEVEN PROVEN PRINCIPLES OF ENTREPRENEURSHIP

WILLIAM F. PICKARD, Ph.D.

with Denise Crittendon

REAL
TIMES
MEDIA

Published in the United States of America by Real Times Media
Real Times Media, 479 Ledyard, Detroit, Michigan 48201, USA.

Library of Congress Cataloging in-Publication Data.
Pickard, William F. Millionaire moves: seven proven principles of entrepreneurship/
William F. Pickard, Ph.D. Other data XX
A catalog entry for this book is available from the Library of Congress.

ISBN 978-1-935601-90-6 (paperback)
ISBN 978-1-935601-93-7 (eBook)

Our books may be purchased in bulk for promotional, educational,
or business use. Please visit our website at
www.makingmillionairemoves.com.

Printed in United States of America and Distributed by CreateSpace.

First Edition: February 2017
10 9 8 7 6 5 4 3 2 1

Book Design by Charles Kreloff

This book is dedicated to my beloved mother, Victoria Woodyard Pickard, my father, Willie Henry Pickard, my beautiful and brilliant daughter, Mary Victoria Pickard, and to the people of LaGrange, Georgia, who often attend Solomon Grove Baptist Church under the leadership of Rev. Hall. Finally, whatever blessings I have received in life came from the gene pools of those hardworking entrepreneurial people known as the Pickards and Woodyards of Troup County Georgia, especially the Woodyards who worshipped at Zion Hill Baptist Church.

ACKNOWLEDGMENTS

I'd like to extend a special shout out to the men of the Alpha Interest Groups as well as the Brothers of Alpha Phi Alpha Epsilon XI from Western Michigan University and the current and former team members of Global Automotive Alliance in several states and the Country of Canada where we do business. I'd also like to thank the 1,000 plus young women and men who have worked at the McDonald's Bearwood Management Company for more than 45 years and who, in essence, became our extended family. Another special thank you goes to Denise Crittendon for working her magic and skillfully putting my ideas and experiences into words. In addition, I'm offering a heart-felt expression of gratitude to the many friends, associates and editorial and marketing professionals who either lent a hand to this project or assisted me in other endeavors. For your hard work, encouragement and/or camaraderie, Reverend Charles G. Adams, Terry Alexander, David Allen, Bill Allen, Don Allen, Charles Allen, William Ashburn, Pat Baker, Dean Percy Barnes, John Barth, Walter Beach III, Bob Beavers, Dean Le-Quita Booth, Melvin Bradley, Bob Brown, Maurene Brown-Smith, Bob Chappell, Paul Cheeks, Markita Choice, Roscoe Coleman, Robert C. Copeland, Donald Davis, Walter Davis, Richard DeVos Sr., Adam Doumbouya, Elaine Dowdell, De Witt Dykes, Richard English, Mike Finney, Eddie Floyd, Diane Freeman, Doris Gamble, Thaddeus Garrett, Allan Gilmore, Benjamin Gordon, Dr. Conrad Graves, Trinita Grayson, Deborah Green-Virgiles, Stevie Green, William Griggs, Rita Haines, James Haines, Chuck

Harvey, Angelo Henderson, Felicia Henderson, Sylvester Hester, Gail Hewitt, Ray Hirschman, Elliott Holland, Carol Hoover, Pat Hoover, Edgar B. Hope, Paul Hubbard Sr., Reverend Jesse L. Jackson, Harry E. Johnson, Jesse E. Johnson, Harold Johnson, Dr. Arthur L. Johnson, John H. Johnson, Carolyn Jones, Judge Damon L. Keith, John W. Kellogg, Jack Kemp, Reverend Dr. Gerald Kisner, Dr. Francis Albert Kornegay, Harold R. Kutner, Melvin Larsen, Petra Lewis, Sam Logan, Donald Lubbers, John Mack, Phil Meek, Terri Moon, Reverend Otis Moss Sr., James Nichols, Roger Penske, Reverend Dr. James C. Perkins, Judson Pickard, Francis Pierce, Arnold Pinkney, Betty Pinkney, Arnold R. Pinkney, Anita Polk, John Popercheck, John Potts, James Randall, Nelly R. Reid, Dr. Marlo Rencher, R.O. Ridgeway, Harry Roberson, James Robinson, Ray Rogal, Dr. Albert Rogers, Lawrence Root, John Sagan, Alvin Schwartz, Dawn Scott-Batts, Pete Short, Martha Jean "The Queen" Steinberg, Frank Stellar, Charlie Strong, Arthur Teele, Greg Trombley, Mary Turner, Abraham Venable, W.O. Walker, Herb Washington, Donald Westley, Bridget Williams, Leroy Woodyard, Robert L. Wright, Bryan Young, and Roger Young, I thank you.

CONTENTS

*POWER*NOTES

For the first 22 years, my life was hell…orphanages, foster care, drugs and stupidity. In the last fifty years (I'm almost 72 now) my life dramatically changed for the better. Why? The relationships I forged with three key people: Nora Jean (my wife), Attorney Williams (Corky, my best friend) and Dr. William Pickard (my close friend, model and coach). Yes, introduce me to your three closest friends, and that will tell me who you are.

I met Bill over 50 years ago as a "principled, but struggling" social worker, not the mega-millionaire, *Black Enterprise 100, Top 10 Entrepreneurs in America*. What drew me to him was his humanity and generosity. At the time, he was leading the local chapter of the Cleveland NAACP, working on his doctorate and thinking entrepreneurially. When I say entrepreneurially, I'm referring to his profound commitment. In everything he did, Bill took ownership and responsibility for results through excellence and collaboration. He is a great leader and follower (a rare and powerful combination). He knows how to effectively work with the "brothers in the hood" and the "corporate captains of America." Bill's reach, range and inherent leadership skills were way beyond his years then, and even now. If that were not enough to change his and my world, he also is a gifted "storyteller" with a loving "sense of humor," grounded in "street smarts," "hustle" and good old-fashioned "common sense."

As you read this book, think of it as a fireside chat of "life lessons" because like entrepreneurship, life is a serious business. The principles and anecdotes shared (spoiler alert) will reinforce your path to excellence, productivity and service, all while keeping you grounded in solid and seasoned advice. Bill is the model of "hustle beats talent when talent doesn't hustle" or "don't do something permanent with someone who might be temporary" or Buy Black, but sell to anybody—all important lessons I have learned from Doc.

There are three realizations that slowly, but surely will seep out when you spend some time with Doc. He is a compassionate capitalist, a "race man" and an alchemist. An alchemist because he is God-centered. Thus, everything he touches turns to gold (uncanny, but true). He is a capitalist with compassion and generosity, not greed at the center of his life and financial success. Why? The many causes he has given to and the HBCUs he has served and supported, are among the most generous examples of giving in Black America. Finally, as a "Race Man" (as I am, for as long as I have known him) Bill's time, talent and treasure have been deeply committed to the upward mobility of scores of people, particularly Black people. When Doc sits at a table, not only does he eat, he brings something to the table, unconditionally. He models the behavior he expects from our people. Bill is a "leader of leaders."

Vivian Pickard, a sophisticated and gorgeous, retired GM executive, is Bill's ex-wife, best friend, companion and advisor. She is a classic example of his high IQ and EQ (Intelligence/Emotional Quotient). Bill clearly understands the power and importance of relationships, cooperation and collaboration at every level and every passage of life. Vivian and Bill continue to add value to each other's lives in spite of what differences occurred along the way. Bill is a team builder who knows how to spot talent everywhere and extract life lessons from every situation. As you read this book, immerse yourself in his principles and stories. Learn the powerful lessons. Read between the lines of the words not spoken, and know that he is instructing us all that the only way to "get" is to "give" and in the end, we must all learn and earn and return.

Thank you, Dr. Pickard for pouring into my life. You mattered.

—George C. Fraser, Ph.D.
CEO, Frasernet, Inc.
Author, Speaker and Entrepreneur

FORWARD

In the 1970s, many minorities who had achieved success in corporations started leaving the C-Suite to become entrepreneurs, some generating revenue greater than $100 million. The auto manufacturing industry led the charge. Ford Motor Co.'s procurement program alone generated more than $1 billion with minority suppliers. It was a good ride for many entrepreneurs who became outstanding business and civic leaders. Sadly, many of those entrepreneurs are no longer in business and I believe this is true for the following five reasons:

1. They did not surround themselves with managers smarter than themselves.

2. They were too rooted in Detroit and dependent on cozy relationships with top management from Ford, Chrysler, and General Motors.

3. They did not diversify into other industries.

4. They did not form strategic partnerships.

5. They did not envision the decline of the auto industry.

Yet, a few did foresee change and adjust their plans. These entrepreneurs grew larger and more profitable, and none was more successful than William Pickard. Pickard did not initially envision becoming an entrepreneur. After getting his master's degree in social work, he sought ways to help the community and those less fortunate than himself. He started his career in Cleveland, working for the Cleveland Urban League as the director of education and later as the executive director of the National Association for the Advancement of Colored People. After receiving his doctorate, Pickard became a McDonald's franchise owner with multiple restaurants in Michigan. Having made such enormous financial strides, he could have stopped at McDonald's. Instead, he chose to invest in minority-owned automobile suppliers. Pickard acquired 51 percent ownership in six firms, merged them, and partnered with others to form the Global Automotive Alliance, his own supplier base. He became one of Michigan's preeminent business leaders and a change agent. In addition to his automotive manufacturing companies, he purchased more McDonald's restaurants and built several successful media, entertainment, and logistics companies.

Understanding the importance of diversification, Pickard acknowledged the risk in the Detroit-based automotive industry. As a result, he moved part of his operation to new manufacturing centers in the South, again forming strategic partnerships with large companies and non-American auto manufacturers. He went on to become a civic leader in Montgomery, Alabama, and other Southern cities.

Ultimately, Dr. Pickard's journey to success as a multimillionaire and generous philanthropist was guided by the seven principles he shares in this book. Pickard survived and grew while others failed because he dreamed big, diversified his business, and formed profitable joint ventures and strategic partnerships. Further, he moved his operations to stronger regions and always reached back to help others. It was a successful strategy implemented by a consummate and prudent business leader. And while Pickard may talk of slowing down, the people who know him well believe this is idle talk. He still has more mountains to climb and this book is a testament to his continuing commitment to community and the next generation. If we had more Pickards, our communities would be stronger and our society richer.

Within the United States and globally, an ever increasing number of young professionals are seeking careers as entrepreneurs. To that end, I would highly recommend that they first read *Millionaire Moves: Seven Proven Principles of Entrepreneurship*. The book is written with humor and an enlightening perspective that inspires and is sure to be appreciated by entrepreneurs of all ages and levels of success, regardless of heritage. Pickard is truly a model for business aspirants all over the world.

—James H. Lowry
Senior Adviser for The Boston Consulting Group
Inaugural member of the Minority Business Hall of Fame

INTRODUCTION

I fully embrace the mantra: "Each one, reach one, teach one." These words get me fired up. They also explain the purpose of this book. This is my way of giving back, and it's my way of saying that whatever I've done, you can do it, too. It doesn't matter who you are—a blue collar worker, an MBA grad, a new business owner, or a student working nights to pay your way through school.

I suspect that each and every one of you is ready to do more than talk a good game. No doubt, you're tired of waiting, hoping, dreaming. You're eager to lace up your track shoes and sprint all the way to the Fortune 500 finish line.

My brother, my sister, I feel you. I know about the challenges. I recognize your frustrations and the dozens of tasks you're juggling. As an up-and-coming entrepreneur, chances are you're trying to identify the right employees, organize your schedule, and find a mentor/confidante—anyone to offer guidance. If you're wise, you're checking out a number of finance options and taking some extra precautions to build your reputation, stabilize your credit, and save.

Consider *Millionaire Moves: Seven Proven Principles of Entrepreneurship* an essential part of that effort. I've packed a lot of advice into these pages and I believe the insights you gain will give you what you need to turn your hustle into a thriving enterprise. Don't get me wrong; I know nothing is foolproof. However, I'm convinced the tools presented here will help you high jump over the next hurdle. Why? Because they did that for me.

I've been where you probably are right now. Whether you're riding the tide of a financial windfall, struggling to pass an economic theory class, or praying to keep your fledgling operation in the black, yep, I've experienced it, too. I've dealt with the smack downs and I've struggled to overcome doubt. But I've also known the surge of unbeatable confidence. In the end, I conquered. I beat the odds. I soared.

That's what distinguishes my message and sets *Millionaire Moves* apart from the rest. There is a surplus of inspirational, how-to-be-a-winner books on the market, and they all claim to have the answers. But the one you're holding in your hands right now is written by someone who knows the proverbial ropes and has taken the risks. I have the balance sheet and net worth to prove it.

I'm Chairman of Global Automotive Alliance, one of the country's leading minority-owned companies and the first minority-owned group of tier-one and tier-two suppliers of plastic parts to the top three automakers in the United States. By 2014, my Alliance had sales of $475 million. Meanwhile, I've been able to hire individuals looking for their first big break and establish internship programs to recruit the next generation of minority employees in plastics processing.

But none of this happened overnight. As someone who has been on his own payroll since the age of 28, I'm the first to admit that it's been a long trek, one that included more than a few frantic days and sleepless nights. It would have been really easy to give up. I had plans to be a social worker, and it would have been much more comfortable for me to do just that—settle for a college degree and a nine-to-five job.

Instead, I chose the path of self-reliance. Of course, that meant I had to deal with my share of skeptics, cynics, and racists. I kept going anyway. The way I see it, haters are just another part of the experience. If you're a person of color, some form of prejudice is going to try to trip you up sooner or later. It's up to you to maneuver around it, under it, over it, or through it.

In *Millionaire Moves*, I have chosen not to dwell on forecasts of discrimination. To explain why I have to reflect on something I learned from Walter Douglas, the former head of New Detroit, a coalition of civil rights and social justice leaders. During a meeting back in the 1980s, someone asked Douglas about the difficulties minorities faced securing business contracts. His response was priceless.

"Racism is like the weather," he said. "On some days you need your overcoat, your scarf, your hat, mittens, and snow boots. Then, there are days when you simply need a heavy sweater or a trench coat."

So, when something or someone tries to block you, button up your jacket and hold tight to your convictions. That's always been the way I roll. I told myself I could do it—and I did. With the exception of a college teaching stint and four combined years working for the Urban League and the NAACP, I have never really considered myself an employee. I became an employer 45 years ago—and I haven't looked back.

Actually, let me correct that statement. I look back occasionally, but when I do I'm reminding myself of lessons learned and using those lessons to encourage those who are following a similar path. Those who are choosing independence. Those free-spirited upstarts like you. I'm a visionary who believes in the potential of anyone with a positive attitude and a great idea. My goal is to show you how to transform that idea into a profitable endeavor.

Are you ready to make it happen? Then turn the page.

—William F. Pickard, Ph.D.

MY ROAD TO SUCCESS

"Work until your idols become your rivals."
—Drake

I t would be fair to say I was kind of tense that brisk, autumn evening. I was the special guest at an annual dinner filled with news reporters and I wasn't quite sure what to expect. All around me, cameras were flashing. And people I didn't even know were praising me and shaking my hand.

After smiling politely and engaging in the usual social banter, I slipped into a seat behind the dais and waited for the program to begin. When it finally started, I felt that charge I always get. You know, that art-of-the-deal adrenalin? I was pumped up, ready to talk business.

But that's not the way the night unfolded.

Instead, I was regaled with a running list of my achievements. I heard about my life, my contributions, and all the hurdles I had leaped. And, there, before an audience of journalists, civic leaders, and elected officials, I was given one of the highest honors of the state—*The Detroit News 2001 Michiganian of the Year Award*, a recognition based on "good works" that elevate the community.

I was elated and, at the same time, still a bit unnerved. For one thing, I prefer being behind the scenes. For another, well, let's just say I didn't quite see myself in the same category as some of the past recipients—internationally known Michiganians like Rosa Parks, Lee Iacocca, Coleman Young, and Aretha Franklin. They were celebrities while I was the chubby kid from a small town in Georgia. Although I'd become a multinational CEO with a portfolio of major enterprises, I was still coming to terms with my rise from humble beginnings. In the years preceding the *Michiganian of the Year* distinction, I had earned a bachelor of arts, a master's in social work, and a doctorate, all the while fending off doubts from those around me.

No one expected me to graduate from college. After all, I was awkward and could barely see without my glasses. I had no idea that, one day, I'd own McDonald's franchises, become co-managing partner of the MGM Detroit Casino or the co-owner of five Black-owned newspapers. Who could have predicted that I would establish an automotive alliance with eight manufacturing plants in the United States and Canada? And who knew that I'd ever be under such a prestigious spotlight, being feted by some of Detroit's finest dignitaries?

As the applause thundered, I overcame my momentary insecurity, stood up proudly, and gazed out at the crowd. Some of my friends were there—Federal Judge Damon J. Keith, Mayor Dennis Wayne Archer, and Arthur and Chacona Johnson, along with my wife, Vivian Rogers Pickard and notables I had just met. I looked at them with a sense of gratitude and respect. These were not the kind of men and women I had encountered in my childhood circle of hard working, blue collar employees, struggling day laborers, hustlers, "numbers men," and slickly-dressed gamblers.

But, as the saying goes, life can change on a dime. This fickle thing we call "everyday living" is chock-full of haphazard twists, poetic ironies, and subtle, hairpin turns. It doesn't matter where you begin. If you work hard enough, the most unfavorable circumstances can become a landslide of sweet victories. All it takes is drive, teamwork, and plain old-fashioned stick-to-itiveness.

In a nutshell, that's the basis of my success and it's the basis of the lessons you're about to explore. Consider this book a comprehensive guide to self-determination, entrepreneurship, and business leadership, replete with instructions on how to dodge the land mines you'll run into along the way. There's no such thing as a shortcut to success. You're either in it to win it and prepared to do whatever it takes, or you're a pushover, the type who runs away when too many obstacles surface, and the road that sprawls ahead is covered with barbed wire and broken glass. If you're the latter, then I suggest one of two things: either put this book down and abandon your dream, or dig in your heels and make a vow that nothing will ever stand between you and the Promised Land.

The chapters that follow are going to show you how to keep that vow. After reading them, you'll know how to tap inner resources you probably didn't know existed. Further, you will have a dynamic business methodology on how to:

- Establish a reliable network.

- Maintain a high level of liquidity.

- Develop multiple income streams.

- Build sustainable wealth.

You also will learn about something I was lucky enough to inherit: common sense. Yes, it's true. Common sense, that so-called basic instinct, is as important as education, flowcharts, and spreadsheets. Thankfully, it landed in my lap at a young age, compliments of my dear old, street-wise, fast-talking Uncle Paul. Now I'm not saying my Uncle Paul was a business genius or that the lessons he imparted are the cornerstone of my achievements. However, I readily acknowledge that his savvy, gut-level insights have had a major impact on my life.

For that reason, I'm passing them on. I'm singing the praises and exposing the strategies of a man known about town for his unbeatable confidence, macho swagger, and a pocket that was always stuffed with money. He was a "numbers man" and, in the 1950s and 1960s, it was no secret how much that meant in the Black community. I got to know him after my parents (Dad worked in the auto plant and Mama was a day worker) moved our family from LaGrange, Georgia, to Flint, Michigan. Eventually, we settled into a lower middle-income neighborhood with a sprinkling of Black businesses, including a record shop owned by Flint boxing legend Larry Watkins.

Larry gave me my first job and exposed me to business techniques that would serve me well later in life. Under his wing, I learned customer relations and the importance of cash flow. Larry also had a unique way of promoting his business. Every Sunday he played nothing but gospel music and, sure enough, the church folks would pile into the store and buy albums featuring James Cleveland, The Soul Stirrers, and others. In those days, we didn't use the term strategic marketing, but that's exactly what Larry was doing. Although I didn't realize it at the time, he and my Uncle Paul were my first real entrepreneurial role models.

Since those years, I've met and been inspired by many high-profile leaders—from Malcolm X to Henry Ford—but when I teach business seminars at colleges around the country, I usually offer this anecdote:

In 1955, a young Black man graduates from the Meharry Medical College School of Dentistry and he's number one in his class. He returns to Detroit and wants to open his dental practice. He needs an office manager, he needs some money, and he needs equipment, and it all comes to $4,500. Where does the money come from?

Inevitably, a few students will answer: "He goes to the bank." Others will shout out: "His family has money." Then I always look at the class and smile.

"No," I reply. "In many cases, his daddy went to the numbers man and then the numbers man loaned him the money. That was our economy. That was our bank. As a rule, in 1955, very few banks would loan a Black man money to open a business."

Next, I tell the class that I could introduce them to undertakers who successfully operated funeral homes for 30 years, but still could not get a bank loan. They were financed by the numbers man. My Uncle Paul not only taught me this, he showed me with his own clever, cool example and a litany of tips. Among them:

"Never try to hustle a hustler."

And "always give the sucker another break."

Those sayings would be most instructive to me later in life, especially when I invested in my first McDonald's franchise.

My favorite?

"Always leave something on the table for the sucker. That way, he'll always come back."

In other words, we're part of an ecosystem. Just as farmers leave corn in the fields to attract deer and other animals to protect their crops, Uncle Paul realized that he needed to ensure that individuals who patronized his establishments returned again and again.

This suggestion intrigued me and—like most of the advice I gained from Uncle Paul—it's now an indelible mark on my mind. I've filed his lessons up there with the best of them—the ones learned at universities and the ones gained in the proverbial School of Hard Knocks.

Yes, I've learned from my successes. But I've learned even more from my failures.

That, perhaps, is one of the most important messages you will glean from my experiences. You'll discover that a rare few people will travel a road that is smoothly paved all the way from the beginning to the end. On your way to business leadership, you'll discover that it's okay to stumble in the process of getting where you want to go. Mistakes happen. In fact, it's a guarantee at some point. The only people who don't mess up are the ones who don't try. It's like that with anything you attempt: a jump shot on the basketball court, a rigorous triathlon, or something as simple as roller skating around a rink. People who skate often get a few scratches and scrapes on their arms and legs. If they don't tumble a few times, that means they didn't attempt any daring new hops or dance moves. They simply played it safe and rolled around and around the rink.

That's not what they're aiming for and neither should you.

If you're serious about becoming an entrepreneur, you're not interested in circling the same route over and over. You're shooting for a higher, faster track, which means you need to take calculated risks. Risk-takers are the ones who move beyond their staid, rank-and-file job and find a way to jump-start their fortune.

For me, that jump-start was a McDonald's franchise. My two partners, Raymond Snowden and Melvin Garrett, and I were among the first African Americans to own a "Mickey D's" in the United States. But like most of my accomplishments, it couldn't have happened without discipline and a strict adherence to my cherished rules. I call them my Seven Proven Principles of Entrepreneurship.

They are:

1. Develop positive **Vision and Attitude**. They represent foresight and the ability to sustain an image of something that has not yet manifested.

2. Be mindful of **Opportunity**. Always search for what's missing and fill the void with ideas and actions.

3. Look for **Finance** options everywhere, starting with your own personal savings account.

4. Build good **Relationships**. They are worth their weight in diamonds.

5. Choose a team with the right **Talent and Skill Set**. They are the foundation of a business.

6. Do not overreact to **Failure**. It's like gravity. Sometimes you fall; all you have to do is get up.

7. Cultivate strong **Faith**. It's the fuse that electrifies, creates new goals, and expands dreams.

These are the keystones that fired up my spirit and enabled me to pursue my first real venture. They are the guidelines I developed and nurtured over the years as I invested in a myriad of enterprises, juggled various businesses, and established multiple streams of income. Along the way, I have grown and so has my entrepreneurial acumen. I have never stopped believing in and cultivating these seven principles.

Who knows where I would be if I hadn't followed them when I took on what I now consider one of the most significant positions of my youth?

The year was 1967 and I was a 27-year-old social worker serving as executive director for the Cleveland branch of the NAACP. The organization was calling for change and leading a boycott against Carling Black Label Beer. A brewery and distribution center in the heart of the Black community, Carling was a supplier for Black bars and restaurants. However, it hired very few Black employees and had no Black delivery truck drivers. The NAACP leadership began meeting with Carling representatives daily.

Meanwhile, my boss and a group of investors brokered an under-the-table deal to become owners of the Carling distributorship in Cleveland. I was shocked. My boss had not considered how the community would be affected by his personal deal, nor had he thought about me. This was my first wake-up call about leadership, politics, and the importance of securing a seat at the bargaining table. It taught me about trust. It showed me that people, even those promoting causes, can be self-serving. And it inspired me to always seize the moment.

Ironically, this strange chain of events would change my life.

At the time, there was a street hustler (who will remain unnamed) in the Black community who was making so much noise about injustice that people began to regard him as an activist. He was outspoken, fiery, and, according to some, had questionable motives. Clearly, he was a force to be reckoned with. He led a group of Black Nationalists and they were some *baaad* brothers. Whenever they placed that red-black-and-green liberation flag in front of a restaurant business would drop by at least 80 percent.

It wasn't long before McDonald's became their target. When the Black Nationalists discovered that not a single Black person had ever owned a McDonald's franchise in the United States, they launched what became known as Operation Black Unity. Of course, this attracted the attention of my NAACP boss and both of us sprang into action. The circumstances that followed exploded into one of the most successful economic boycotts in the history of the Civil Rights Movement and became a pivotal part of my journey to financial independence.

Throughout the boycott, I maintained the **vision** and belief in the possibility of a Black franchise owner (Principle One), worked diligently and took advantage of **opportunities** (Principle Two), understood the importance of **finance** (Principle Three), developed **relationships** (Principle Four), sought out **talent** (Principle Five), prepared for **failure** (Principle Six), and had unswerving **faith** (Principle Seven) in things working out for the higher good of our community.

So several years later, when I received a call from the McDonald's regional office in Columbus, Ohio, I wasn't totally surprised. And I wasn't afraid of the challenge, especially since the U.S. Small Business Administration was guaranteeing 75 percent of the loan. Because I was working on my doctorate at the time, I took out a student loan for my portion of the down payment and Ray Snowden and Melvin Garrett, my friends and franchise business partners, came up with the rest—a total of $25,000 in equity.

Now, some who are reading this might be tempted to describe this situation as a dash of luck and a touch of providence. Others might use labels like destiny and fate. I have another way of looking at it. I perceive luck as something that happens when preparation collides with opportunity. I reject the notion that our lives are ruled by an unyielding force called destiny and I never take a fatalistic approach to anything. What I do believe in is laying the groundwork, staying the course, and blazing trails for those who will one day fill my shoes.

I'm bragging a little bit, but my company did almost a half-billion dollars in sales in 2015 and landed in the number eight spot on the *Black Enterprise Top 100 Black Businesses* list. I employ nearly 3,000 people and a lot of them look like me. I'm inviting you to join me. In the chapters that follow, you will find a breakdown of my Seven Proven Principles. No, they are not easy. And no, they are not going to reward you with instant wealth. But if you thoroughly study them and apply them accordingly, I'm sure you'll find them as indispensable as I do. They will mold you and help you stay afloat in the rough-and-tumble world of free enterprise.

They will serve as your road map, now, and for many years to come.

PRINCIPLE ONE: VISION & ATTITUDE

*"You can never cross the ocean until you have
the courage to lose sight of the shore."*
—Anonymous

She scrubbed clothes all day long and sometimes half the night. Still, the young washerwoman—a former sharecropper from the Louisiana Delta—barely earned enough to make ends meet. She was a recent widow, so broke and stressed that her hair was falling out. Her scalp itched something fearsome and every time she scratched, it bled. She coped by smearing it with a peculiar-smelling ointment, handmade from her own secret ingredients.

Thus began the powerful mission of Madam C. J. Walker, the nation's first Black female millionaire. Many people have heard her rags-to-riches story and many are aware of the national beauty company she built in the early 1900s. But not everyone knows that it took more than long hours, tireless work—and the invention of the straightening comb—to catapult her to success. Her extraordinary achievements were rooted in her indomitable spirit and a concept that many take for granted. It's called vision.

Vision is foresight and the ability to sustain an image of something that has not yet manifested. It's the 200-unit apartment tower you expect to develop. It's that chain of neighborhood laundromats you sometimes daydream about. It's the business that grosses $100 million annually and maintains a global clientele.

It's the thing you focus upon with the intention of bringing it into existence.

You have to be able to see that perfect credit score; you have to picture yourself walking into the bank and depositing that seven-figure check. You absolutely have to believe it and keep your thoughts aligned with your goal. For instance, I can ask one person, "How are you doing today?" and hear back, "I'm alright," versus another person's response: "It's a great day! I'm glad to be up. I'm going to make something happen."

That's where attitude comes into play. Vision and attitude are like yin and yang. The vision you are holding is actually based on the attitude you have been nourishing. You see, attitude is the emotion that gives birth to your desires and propels you forward. It's the perspective that fuels your imagination and enables you to see things today that will transform your business tomorrow. When you become a visionary, you learn to adjust your lens and shift your perceptions, especially the images you have of yourself.

I know this firsthand. In high school, I didn't consider myself a scholar and I never excelled in sports. I used to hang out with the "losers" club that ate lunch under the staircase and did just enough homework to get by. Luckily for me, one of my teachers, Helen Steele, decided to push me beyond my self-imposed boundaries. She approached me one day after my

English class and spoke to me quite bluntly.

"You have a good mind," she said. "Why don't you use it?"

At first, I was baffled. *A good mind? Me?* I thought she had lost it. Yet a little voice deep inside of me toyed with the idea that she might actually be right. Her words sort of hovered and danced around my spirit. I delighted in flipping through my textbooks after that, and I read them with a little more zeal. I even started to walk differently. I don't know if I ever told Ms. Steele this, but her statement shook me out of my complacency and marked a turning point in my academic years. I became more assertive. My curiosity was piqued and, before long, Ms. Steele's accusatory question became the seed for a new and positive self-image. My doubts had waned and I was beginning to see beyond my narrow parameters.

Hip-hop artist and business mogul, Jay Z, put it this way: "Your vision must be greater than the window you're looking through."

Now that's profound when you think about it. It sums up my situation as a youth and captures the plight of so many young men of color. A young man staring out of a small, obstructed window in Brooklyn's Marcy Projects probably can't see much with his eyes, but his mind can help him peer around the corner, across the bridge, and into the future.

And so it was with Madam C. J. Walker. Others may have viewed her as a poor, uneducated colored woman. But that's not the way she viewed herself. She imagined wealth, luxury, exquisite garments. She pushed her immediate circumstances out of her mind and refused to dwell on the pain of her past. She looked ahead instead of looking back.

To keep her thoughts flowing in the right direction, she

knew she needed support. So she found a piece of plywood and covered it with pictures she'd cut out of a Sears, Roebuck & Co. catalog. She nailed the wood, which she called her "wish board," to the wall of the bedroom she shared with her 11-year-old daughter, Lelia. Every night, she and Lelia would glance at the images before falling asleep. They'd see them again in the morning as they dressed.

This practice is known today as creative visualization and poster boards, vaguely similar to the wooden one used by Madam Walker, are all the rage. These days, they've been dubbed "vision boards," which is a trendy buzz term for a personal montage of photos, affirmations, and magazine clippings that reflect an individual's greatest aspirations. It's an effective tool for training the mind and keeping it riveted on ultimate victory.

However, the creative visualization or the visioning process doesn't begin or end with this technique. Successful people have admitted that they often take time out of their busy schedules just to kick back in their offices, their cars, or homes, imagining themselves in a more exciting setting. In fact, I've done this myself. Years ago, my business partners and I opened a McDonald's in Detroit on Woodward Avenue, one of the longest and busiest streets in the city. I still remember that moment, even though I wasn't experiencing the thrill in the same manner as everyone else. While the aroma of burgers wafted through the restaurant and my business cohorts were giving each other high fives, I was flirting with images of our next venture. Physically, I was under the golden arches on Woodward, but in my mind, I was scouting out a new site in neighboring Highland Park and picturing yet another one on Eight

Mile Road. Eventually, those sites and more materialized, nine to be exact. But by then, I was contemplating another future project.

It's not that I wasn't interested in being in the moment. I'm just not the kind of person who gets stuck on the main attraction. In my head, I have already moved on. And why not? If I never see anything else, then there will never be anything else. This is one of the chief reasons a number of companies are incorporating creative visualization sessions into their leadership and management workshops. It's a method of prodding their employees to reach higher and be more productive. It forces them out of their comfort zone and creates a template for growth.

Like vision boards, creative visualization—which I like to think of as vision that's so hot it's on fire—is as foolproof as gravity and other scientific laws. This method works so well that even Olympic athletes are trying it. They practice incessantly, but they also spend 15 to 20 minutes three or more times a week picturing themselves performing the feat they expect to master. The same for the U.S. Navy Seals. To survive as a Navy Seal, one must be able to remain calm during episodes of intense terror. These men and women endure a rigorous, back-breaking boot camp and deprivation that would make the average person faint. But one of the most critical components of their preparation is a mental toughness training that includes visualization strategies.

Let's stop and mull that over for a minute. Am I implying that you should spend valuable time rearranging the familiar pictures that have settled in your mind? The answer is an unequivocal "yes." The brain is a source of power and that power is deeper and far more expansive than simply memorizing facts and adding up numerical figures. Business sense doesn't end with your management skills and your ability to organize a successful financial campaign or PowerPoint presentation. As Albert Einstein once explained, "Imagination is more important than knowledge. Knowledge is limited to all we now know and understand, while imagination embraces the entire world and all there ever will be to know and understand."

Here are 11 tips that will help you get in that visionary frame of mind:

DRAW STRENGTH FROM YOUR SQUAD

Make your friends your brain trust. Bouncing and vibing off each other creates a synergy. Henry Ford, Harvey Firestone, and Thomas Edison knew this and used it to their advantage. When they came together, ideas flowed and the magic of their collective genius was ignited. Former Detroit Mayor Dennis W. Archer, Ronald E. Hall Sr., CEO of Bridgewater Interiors, Roy S. Roberts, Group Vice President of General Motors, and I shared a similar bond and it contributed to our combined success. In some circles, this is known as masterminding. Individuals in mastermind groups get together and hold the vision for one another. They discuss one another's highest hopes and each of them encourages the other to recalibrate their thoughts and take them to the next level. Multimillion-dollar deals have coalesced, all because a mastermind group saw them signed, sealed, and delivered.

FANTASIZE

If you're only thinking about what is currently going on in your life, you're already out of focus. Don't allow reality to completely dictate your reality. Every now and then, forget about the road-blocks that surround you and imagine what you want. Seriously, try it. For this exercise you don't have to close your eyes, but you must ignore images of what's annoying you and replace them with vibrant scenes of what you desire. If you can, try to add some emotion. Feel the joy and enthusiasm of landing that promotion or finalizing that multimillion-dollar deal.

LET GO OF YESTERDAY

Never let bygones control you. Learn from your mistakes and/or the hurts others may have caused. Then release them. If you waste too much time gazing in the rearview mirror, you might become bitter, unmotivated, and depressed. In the process, you'll miss the greater gifts that lie ahead. As our ancestors used to say, "Keep your eyes on the prize." A person with vision understands that thinking too much about the drama of the past is like stepping into quicksand. You get pulled in. And, if you don't get out in time, you sink. It's best to avoid that trap. Look forward and march onward. As author and business leader Stephen Covey says, "Live out of your imagination and not your history."

BE SERIOUS ABOUT SAVING

People with a poverty mentality are mired in materialism because they have a fake-it-because-you'll-never-make-it mantra running through their brains. They don't have anything and they never expect to have anything. For them, the only way to feel good is to spend every dime on designer clothes and other adornments that create a façade about their financial well-being. But if you're stashing money away, you're embracing the possibilities. Savings are an indication that you're looking toward the future, which is a key component to having a vision and holding it. You're not one of the "sheeple" who graduate from college, get a job and spend, go to work and buy, get up the next day and spend again, then buy, spend, and buy. You've broken from the visionless cycle of living for the weekend. You understand the adage: "Wealthy people teach their children how to acquire. Rich people teach their children how to sell. Poor people teach their children how to buy."

BE FLEXIBLE

There's a reason for tradition and there's also room for new ideas, but the tightrope that binds the two can be a bit wobbly. It's up to you to learn how to balance on it. In other words, you have to decide if you want to bend and cooperate or go against the status quo. My partners and I discovered this paradox one March when McDonald's rolled out a new Shamrock Shake for St. Patrick's Day. We didn't believe Black people would drink Shamrock Shakes. Because it was the 1970s and the height of the Black Power Movement, we hired a guy to wear a gorilla suit. Please forgive our ignorance for thinking that this reflected our African heritage. Luckily, there was also someone there dressed like the happy-faced icon, Ronald McDonald. All the kids rushed to him and we couldn't make enough green Shamrock Shakes to keep up with the demand from our Black customers. Oh well, that's how you learn!

BE AN OPTIMIST

Have you heard the one about the optimist who goes hunting with a pessimist? The pessimist is trudging along, moping, and the optimist is bounding down a woodsy trail, proudly showing off his beautiful golden retriever. When the two men reach a river, the optimist picks up a stick and throws it as far as he can. The golden retriever jumps in and actually runs across the top of the water. The pessimist doesn't say a word. So, the optimist does it again. He picks up a stick and tosses it into the rippling river. Once again, the dog walks on the water and fetches the stick. The pessimist looks bored and the optimist can't take it anymore. He looks at the pessimist and asks: "Don't you see anything unusual about my dog?" The pessimist glares at him. "Sure I do," he snarls. "He can't swim!" Okay so it's a corny joke, but it adequately summarizes the differences in the way people approach life. It's not what's happening to you, it's the meaning you give to what is happening to you. Your perspective can help you rise up or it can yank you back to the ground. It is all up to you. Are you concentrating on examples of triumph or thinking about a couple of friends who launched small businesses and failed? Are you scouring your circumstances for opportunities and second chances? Or pondering everything that could go wrong? Do you see the miracles or do you see dogs that can't swim?

QUIET TIME

Here's an anonymous quote that I think is pretty powerful. It states, "Quiet, calm deliberation disentangles every knot." This means that solutions are rarely found in the midst of pandemonium. If you're trying to solve a problem or figure out your next step, it's best to retreat to a silent place. It could be your dorm room (if it's possible to find quiet there) or your apartment (minus the girlfriend, the roommate, and the blaring music). Perhaps, you could try a chapel, a park, or a quiet corner of the library. Whatever spot you choose, use that time and space to go inside. That's where the messages are buried and it's usually the only time those subtle inner voices will come out from hiding. Whether you're praying, meditating, or doing nothing in particular, that peaceful repose will help you clear your mind. You'll get ideas. You'll make decisions. You'll know which deals to consider and which ones to pass up. And you artistic types, take note: Smokey Robinson, who is considered one of the greatest songwriters of all time, wrote some of his best music while relaxing in his bathtub.

TRAVEL

Get out, see the world, but remember this: When you're traveling, you're taking time out to rest your body. But, that doesn't mean you have to shut down your mind. Entrepreneurial vision never takes a holiday. Whether you're touring the ruins of Rome or climbing the pyramids of Egypt, keep scanning your surroundings for hints. Some friends and I were traveling through Mexico when I saw my first Jiffy Lube concept. I went bonkers over the idea. As soon as I returned to the United

States, one of my business partners and I opened up one that did exceptionally well financially. I credit my trip for the exposure and stimulation. Nothing revs up your vision like travel. When you're outside of your typical humdrum existence, you're introduced to different ways of thinking and being. The sights you see often spark questions which can, in turn, place your life on a whole new trajectory. My buddy, Ray Snowden, is the best proof I have of this. He landed a job as busboy on a cruise ship when he was only 17. The ship took him on a magnificent journey on the Great Lakes through Niagara Falls, Buffalo, Chicago, and Milwaukee. Ray was able to meet rich people and observe their way of life. As a result, he became fanatical about etiquette, all the way down to how you eat your soup. Soon, he began to adopt the lifestyle and behave like this had always been part of his world.

READ

Knowledge is power. Read publications like *The Wall Street Journal*, *The New York Times*, *The Entrepreneur*, *Black Enterprise*, and *The Washington Post*. You'll gain a great deal of information and gather idea after idea. I set aside two to three hours a night just for reading. I enjoy some articles and books so much I re-read them, discuss them with colleagues, and recommend them to students. One example is the popular *Rich Dad, Poor Dad* by Robert Kiyosaki. According to Kiyosaki, the dad with a college degree and a government job that paid quite well didn't achieve nearly as much as the real estate agent dad who was always selling and buying. Although the salesman dad didn't graduate from college, he became much richer than the one who did. I also recommend *Why "A" Students Work for "C" Students and "B" Students Work for the Government*, also by Kiyosaki. Both books offer motivational messages that mirror one of my core beliefs: To achieve mega success, you don't have to be the sharpest knife in the drawer. But you have to be double-dog daring. You have to have moxie, grit, and chutzpah.

HIT THE RESET BUTTON

The bad news is that a lousy mood can affect your attitude and impact your job performance. The good news is that, no matter what's going on, you have the power to change how you're feeling. Instantly. Just repeat an encouraging quote, an inspirational expression, or a snappy line from a song that makes you smile. It could be something fun like Bruno Mars' "I'm smoother than a fresh jar of Skippy." Or it could be the Reverend Jesse Jackson's emphatic, "I am somebody!" If you find yourself in a state-of-mind that isn't resourceful, quietly say or sing a positive message to yourself. Whenever I meet a person who is having a rough day, I never allow myself to get drenched in their shower of negativity. I say to myself: "You don't have the power to destroy my joy." That's my reset button.

WATCH QUALITY TELEVISION

Oh, I know some readers are wondering how something as seemingly inane as television made this list. Easy. Because it's not the TV that's the problem, it's what people are watching. If you turn to Public Television, you can learn about history, space, or politics. On CNN, you'll get news from across the planet. Meanwhile, C-SPAN reviews books on certain days. On other networks, reporters rove around the country wandering through remote villages, museums, and castles. Just because you have a TV doesn't mean you have to watch crazy, mindless programming. Black folks watch more TV per capita per hour than any group in America, but a significant number of us are watching junk. What does this have to do with vision? Simple. You will never be what you cannot see.

The bottom line is this: You must see doors where there are no doors. A leader with vision observes promise in the dust—an abandoned house, a vacant lot, an empty garage in a rundown, inner-city neighborhood. Some of us grew up in tattered houses, while others were raised in sleek homes in the 'burbs. There's beauty in all of it because, from it, you might be able to sift out memories that could morph into opportunities. You can take the stuff you learned on the streets, clean it up, shine it up, and make it useful to you in a professional context. For example, the Super Soaker, invented by Black nuclear engineer Lonnie Johnson, is no more than an oversized water gun with lots of splash power. I know Johnson personally, and like the rest of us, he used to spend the summers of his childhood chasing his friends with one of those puny, easy-to-break, plastic squirt guns. While the rest of us lamented the limitations of our pretend weapons, he did something about it. Within two years, his ingenious toy had generated $200 million in retail sales.

That's the lesson. If you've grasped it, then you're almost ready for the next step. Before you move on, let's go over a few of the pitfalls you'll need to avoid. I call these The Vision Busters.

DON'T Confuse Vision With Living Beyond Your Means. Yes, in order to be it, you have to see it. But don't stretch your imagination so far beyond your budget that you end up in a financial bind. What you integrate into your life has to be filtered and tempered. If not, things can get out of hand. Most risks are planned and calculated. Even a dreamer has to seek balance and know when to act and when to wait.

DON'T Leap Before You Look. Not every business belongs in every location. Do your homework and assess whether or not an opportunity is ideal for the venue you have in mind. I know a guy who went to California and saw Roscoe's Chicken restaurant. He came back and announced that he was going to open several Roscoe's in Detroit. I highly advised him against it. Unlike McDonald's or Popeye's, which are backed by a corporation that allow them to become national and international chains, Roscoe's is a local, small-chain business that doesn't transfer well to other cities. He didn't listen. His three or four Roscoe restaurants only lasted a year.

DON'T Get in a Familiarity Rut. Step out of your comfort zone. I've met a number of young business owners who are afraid to stray too far from their roots. They can't think beyond the traditional soul food diner or barbecue shack. This need for familiarity breeds a lack of vision. In 1980, one of the top players at Motorola began experimenting with new communications technology and invited me to join in on their efforts to take cell phones national. But, again, this was 1980. I had never heard of, much less seen, a cell phone. The concept was too abstract and alien. I knew about food operation, not burgeoning technology. Because I clung to the familiar, I didn't develop the vision I needed to get in on the ground floor of a sector that was about to explode.

DON'T Get Drunk On Success. There's an old saying, "Money doesn't change people. It reveals them." If you're a jerk while you're broke, you're going to be an even bigger jerk when you attain wealth. My Jiffy Lube business partner got so carried away by all the success we were enjoying he violated our agreement and started another franchise in another state—without me. He added a few more and made so much money he couldn't spend it. Then his son got involved and ended up addicted to drugs. Soon, all the money was gone.

One of my favorite quotes is from Helen Keller, an author and political activist who was deaf, blind, and mute. She said "The only thing worse than being blind is having sight but not vision." The groundwork for vision is laid when you wake up from society's restrictions on what you can and cannot accomplish. Sometimes, that means doing something no one else has ever attempted. For instance, Bob Johnson was working for the Federal Communications Commission (FCC) when he stumbled upon information that would revolutionize the world of television. While reading the FCC rules and regulations, he came across a regulation that said underserved communities are eligible for certain opportunities. Johnson went to Viacom with his idea for Black Entertainment Television (BET). He was an upstart who introduced the entertainment industry to a market that had long been neglected.

What ideas do you have? What obscure bit of information

caught your eye today? Are there potential breakthroughs percolating inside of you? You are the mover and the shaker who can make it all happen by learning to see with something other than your eyes.

Perhaps Mary McLeod Bethune embodies this best. When Ms. Bethune, an educator, activist and lecturer, decided she wanted to build a vocational school for colored girls in Winterhaven, Florida, she remembered that Harvey Firestone, Henry Ford and Thomas Edison wintered there every year. She also knew the Negro chauffeur who drove them. After a few efforts, she was able to persuade this chauffeur to bring the three moguls to the parcel of land that would be the site of her new school.

She led them to an empty field, the site of a former city dump.

"I've got my dorms, my girls learning canning and how to be nurses," she said

Ford, Firestone, and Edison quietly gazed out at the barren land. Then Ford leaned over to his two friends and whispered: "You think she's a little feeble?"

They didn't answer for a while and Ms. Bethune continued her tour.

Finally, one of the men called out: "Ms. Bethune, where is this facility?"

She held her head high and responded: "In my mind."

PRINCIPLE TWO: OPPORTUNITY

"When someone tells me no it doesn't mean I can't do it.
It simply means I can't do it with them."
—Karen E. Quinones Miller

In the early 1900s, hotels didn't allow non-whites. Neither did restaurants and most gas station restrooms. So it wasn't unusual for African American travelers to pack a couple of day's worth of sandwiches and drive all night without stopping. If the journey became too rigorous, they simply pulled alongside the highway and slept in the car.

Then in 1936, a New York City postman decided he couldn't take it anymore. Victor H. Green reached out to other mailmen in his network and used their input to compile a listing of African American households that were renting out rooms. His handy little guide was known as *The Negro Motorist Green Book,* and it was not only valuable, it was a necessity. If you were Black and ready to hit the road, Brother Green's book was your Bible. He may not have fully realized it at the time but, in his state of frustration, he had stumbled upon that empty oasis all entrepreneurs seek: the realm of opportunity.

A vital resource was born, all because Green was fed up. Opportunities are like that. They're not always rare. They're seldom complicated. They're not even that hard to find. Often, they're like *The Green Book* – the answer to a problem that's right in front of your eyes.

But it's up to you to wake up and take heed. After all, we're living in America, touted as the land of opportunity. This is not the place where people flee so they can scratch their heads and complain that they have no idea how to make money or how to find the doorway to their dreams. If you turn on the six o'clock news, you'll see and hear about a different outlook. While many of us lament that America has seen its best days and grumble about jobs being outsourced to Mexico and Asia, others are devising schemes to get here, and get ahead.

Sadly, many of them end up becoming statistics; drowning off the coast of Florida or dehydrating in overheated, poorly-ventilated trucks. But their desperation to reach the Free World suggests there's still something on these shores that's makes it worth their while. It's an indication that the economy may have shifted, and banks may not be shelling out big loans, but movers are still moving and shakers are still shaking. It just depends on your focus.

Case in point: When I was in college, one of my roommates was from Uganda and he had the oddest comb I'd ever laid my eyes on. It was made out of wood and shaped like a wide fork with a stubby handle. Every time he used this comb to groom his hair, I cracked up. Five years later, almost every Black person in America had a plastic version of that *afro pick*. Instead of laughing at my African homie, I should have seen the handwriting on the wall. My former roommate filled a need that I ignored. Later in life when I traveled to Africa, you better believe I saw business opportunities everywhere and when I returned to the United States, I was prepared to act on them.

It's sort of like a riddle. All you need to do is survey your own surroundings and ask yourself what's missing. While you're complaining about the loss of homegrown opportunities you might be allowing local and international possibilities to slip through your fingers. Think about it for a moment. In 1945, when John H. Johnson launched Ebony Magazine, there were very few publications that catered to Black interests. He filled a void. When 21-year-old Ludwick Marishane of South Africa—named Global Student Entrepreneur of the Year in 2011—created a lotion that cleanses the body without water, he filled a void for 2.5 billion people worldwide who lack access to clean water and a sanitary means of bathing.

How about you? What was that last concern you expressed while strolling through your community? Do you see any potential there? What about your friends? Are any of them yearning for a service, an item, a specific brand of clothing? Are your fellow students complaining about anything that you think you can provide?

Once, I spoke at a historically Black college in Alabama and gave the students the same advice I'm sharing here. One young man reacted in a big way. He noticed that some of the neighboring universities had a population of students who were a bit more affluent than those at the school he attended. Many of those well-heeled students, particularly the freshmen, were fretting over the inconvenience of having to do their own laundry.

The young man sprung into action. He began driving from campus to campus, posting flyers about his laundry pick-up business. Later, he drove to the dorms on those campuses, picked up clothes, delivered them to laundry service centers and returned them—fresh and clean. His company was an instant success. Why? Because one person's curse can be another man's or woman's blessing.

It's all about keeping an open mind. It's all about digging for gold instead of pointing at obstacles. It's all about doing what Booker T. Washington used to preach. During his many lectures, he would encourage his audience to "cast down your bucket where you are." Today that could translate into a pet grooming business, an on-campus manicure service, a soul food diner near your grandma's church. Or it might mean scrutinizing something outdated and adding a few modern tweaks. I don't know the last time you rode in a cab, but when Uber entered the scene, the transportation business changed overnight. These days, when I give talks at colleges I ask students how many taxi cabs Uber owns. The answer, of course, is none. Uber is the perfect example of a company that is revolutionizing an industry and practically turning it upside down. It's the largest taxi service in America, yet it doesn't own a single vehicle.

Tell me, how can you be in the transportation business and not own any cars? That's unheard of, isn't it? Well, let's examine its foundation. What's Uber's business model? *Use Your Own Car!* That means if you're a taxi cab owner in New York City you have paid anywhere from $450,000 to $700,000 for a taxi medallion. Now Uber comes to town and anyone with a late model car in good working order can pick up people and knock you out of the game.

Airbnb follows a similar path and process. With access to more than two million homes worldwide, it's altering the tradition of hotels as we once knew them. The irony is that when Brother Green was locating accommodations for our mamas, daddies, and grandparents, he was running an Airbnb, old-school style. But he had an unusual goal for an entrepreneur. Green dreamed of a day when his business model would no longer be necessary. By the time he died in 1960, he was pretty close to getting his wish. After the passage of the 1964 Civil Rights Act, Jim Crow laws were gradually abolished and American hotels and restaurants began opening up to people of color. Although *The Green Book* expanded beyond New York and eventually included most of North America, his family didn't continue it. It is now a faded chapter in Black history, a reminder of the ingenuity of African Americans making a way out of no way.

Yet, it's still the original business model for what has become a growing practice of conducting successful enterprises without the brick and mortar. I call the new, non-traditional businesses cyberspace babies. They take emerging technologies and figure out how to marry them with old concepts. For millennial entrepreneurs, the possibilities are infinite. But how do you sift through this sea of trends and come up with something even more innovative? Let's count the ways:

ADAPT OLD IDEAS TO THE LATEST TECHNOLOGY

What did Uber really bring to the party? Cars were already there. People were already there. Uber brought technology. The company created an app. If you're paying attention, you realize that technology is impacting everything and you're probably wondering where else it can be included and how it can be applied. All you have to do is ask the right questions. How is it that the University of Phoenix is one of the largest for-profit universities in the United States, but most of its classes are online? If you see a business lagging behind the times, create something similar but more technologically-efficient. Or maybe you can launch a service that shows an existing business how to integrate technology into their services. A number of pizza spots figured this out sometime ago. Domino's, Papa John's and Little Caesar's, for instance, allow customers to order via Twitter, email, text message, and smart watch. That's what I call staying abreast of the times.

IMPROVE WHAT'S ALREADY THERE

McDonald's owner Ray Kroc was a musician. Let me say that again. The man responsible for the largest restaurant chain in the world made a living as a performing artist. He supplemented his income by working as a salesman for a company that manufactured the multi-mixers that are used in shake machines. After a while, he began to notice something interesting. He sold more cups for these machines to a small restaurant in a California town called San Bernardino than anywhere else in the country. Curiosity got the best of him and Kroc made it his business to find out why. He flew to California to meet with the McDonald brothers and discovered that they were doing a brisk business selling nothing but burgers, fries, soft drinks, and shakes. The line wrapped around the corner. Intrigued, Kroc asked the brothers if they wanted to expand and take their vision across the country. They weren't interested but allowed Kroc to develop the plan and pay them 1 percent of the sales. Eventually, Kroc bought them out completely and the popular eatery exploded into the international chain that millions of people frequent today.

PRACTICE "TWO-ARMED" LIVING

I can't take credit for this one. It belongs to my witty, high-spirited granddaddy. Whenever someone had a job and recognized opportunities to do business with those he worked with, my granddaddy used the "two-armed living" expression. It's actually a pretty inventive approach to business. For instance, I know of a schoolteacher who taught shop, carpentry, and auto mechanics. Half of the employees at the school were women and many of them were single. In their apartments, they needed shelves installed, pictures mounted, and more. So the shop teacher used his own resources to create a carpentry business on the side. While the other teachers drove standard cars, he made so much money he bought a canary yellow Corvette.

MAKE ALL SITUATIONS SERVE YOU

What did we do before Post-it® Notes? We jotted things down haphazardly, here or there. It was a hodge-podge system that led to a lot of lost messages and one big mess. Enter Arthur Fry, an engineer for 3M, formerly known as the Minnesota Mining and Manufacturing Co. He was also active in his church and fond of his role of singing in the choir. But he was constantly frustrated by page markers that kept slipping out of place, making it hard for him to find the right songs in his hymnal. It seemed silly at first, but he decided to try some of the adhesive created by his colleague, Spencer Silver. Voila! Although the adhesive had been deemed a failure at 3M, it was the perfect solution to Fry's problem. He returned to the office and explained that, when used properly, the glue was quite functional. By making the best of an awkward situation, Fry came up with a clever little item that many companies now consider an essential tool. Post-it® Notes are one of the top five best-selling office supply products in the world.

BE OBSERVANT

Some people think of people-watching as a mindless activity. I know of someone who did it so much he discovered an opportunity. He was an employee at a small regional airport when he noticed that nothing upset travelers more than losing their luggage. After he retired, he contacted a friend who served on the aviation committee for the board of the city's airport authority. His friend gave him an inside scoop on how to bid on contracts to deliver lost bags. The retired guy bid and got nowhere. He tried again the next year, the next year, and then again the year after. Finally, after years of persistence, he landed a contract that allowed him to pick up misplaced bags and deliver them to distraught travelers. It turned into a profitable business with low overhead. All he needed was an SUV, a tank of gas, and four or five buddies who wanted to make extra money on the side.

FIND AN UNMET NEED AND FILL IT

I live in a community that has a special arrangement with the police department. If a resident goes out of town, he or she can leave keys and information about their whereabouts so that the police can provide special security at their home. One day, one of the officers knocked on my door and said he was planning to retire and launch a business that was more extensive than the standard police department patrols. For a fee, the retired officer would make daily surveillances inside the homes of people who would be away for an extended period of time. Well, several years ago the pipes burst in my home's steam sauna. However, very little damage occurred because the officer caught it on the second day. Sometimes, I'm gone for an extended period of time. My house could have been a total wreck. This business filled an important need.

EXAMINE RESTAURANT MENUS

Vegetarian restaurants have been around for awhile, but who would have thought restaurants would exist that catered specifically to vegans, people who eat no meat or animal by-products, including dairy and eggs? And who would have thought that you could walk into a major chain restaurant and ask for gluten-free food? Soon, we will have restaurants that are entirely gluten-free. If you're interested in opening a food establishment, study the trends and determine where there's a demand and/or an untapped niche.

SUBSCRIBE TO FLIPBOARD

Flipboard is an online tool, or app, and is one of the best ways to get ideas, inspiration, and updates on what's going on in the world. To subscribe, simply answer a set of questions about your preferred topics of interest and Flipboard takes it from there. The company surveys over 500 magazines a day and will email you articles that pertain to your key concerns. It's the fastest way to stay motivated, get a behind-the-scenes look at emerging new opportunities and gather the facts you need to make definitive decisions.

FOLLOW YOUR PASSION

I'm sure you've tried Mrs. Fields Cookies at least once in your life. But did you know she started out as a California housewife who enjoyed whipping up batches of cookies and selling them around her subdivision in Palo Alto? She even went to banks with fresh cookie samples and a business plan. But the bankers would eat all of her cookies and refuse her loan request. After being continually denied a bank loan that would have helped her purchase ovens, Mrs. Fields thought about the fact that most churches had kitchens but only used their ovens once or twice a week. She contracted with 30 churches before finally securing a loan with 21 percent interest. Today, Mrs. Fields Famous Brands, parent to the TCBY Yogurt and Mrs. Fields Cookie chains, has more than 650 retail outlets, over 300 franchises, and a net worth of $65 million.

No matter what route you take, remember one thing: Ingenuity is the midwife of opportunity. This is one of my most fervent beliefs. I don't believe in the word "no" and I have the utmost respect for go-getters like Ray Kroc, Victor Green, and Mrs. Fields. As James Brown used to sing: "I don't want nobody to give me nothing. Open up the door and I'll get it myself."

It just so happens that some people were at the right door at the right time. I was one of those people. My friends and I were probably the ninth Black group in the country to open a new McDonald's franchise. That was a huge feat. And it's a milestone I might not have been able to reach in a different country and at a different point in history.

It's a well-known fact that in certain parts of the world, if your daddy was a butcher, you would more than likely become a butcher. Not so in the United States. My father was a good man, but he never achieved a fraction of the success I have obtained and I believe that may be due, in part, to a special "door" that opened and allowed me to "get it myself." I'm not diminishing my credentials. But I honestly don't feel a Bill Pickard-type would have become owner of a McDonald's franchise without a fleeting moment in time labeled Affirmative Action.

Affirmative Action is a government and private sector program created in response to a lopsided and unfair playing field in a country that had denied opportunities to Blacks for centuries. When I came along, there was a great deal of pressure from Black political leaders like Detroit Mayor Coleman Young to open up opportunities for Black suppliers, dealers, foremen, and apprentices. Note that I have never viewed Affirmative Action as a plan based on quotas. It was no more a quota system than Harvard or Yale's archaic admission policies of the past. If they had admitted students based on test scores, Asians would have made up 40 percent to 60 percent of the population. That's what I say to people who try to suggest that Affirmative Action and quotas are synonymous. If those same individuals are so opposed to quotas, then why do they support legacy admissions at a large number of institutions, including some of the top universities in the country?

The bottom line is that certain individuals were given a boost, and I was one of them. In America, the doors of opportunity swung open around 1968. If you could walk, talk, and chew bubble gum as a proactive Black person, you had a good chance of boarding the train that led to the right jobs, loans, grants, and business contracts. If you had that same level of ambition in the 1950s, it didn't matter. African Americans were still being relegated to the lowest rung of the social ladder. Back then, some Black women with bachelor's degrees landed jobs as teachers. But many were working as domestics while Black men with similar backgrounds were working in the post office.

Fortunately, that era was replaced by two decades of Affirmative Action, business set asides, and other incentives. Unfortunately, those days are gone. When the 2008 financial crisis and recession swept the country, cutbacks ensued and the landscape of abundance began to shrink. In 1966, if you knocked on the door of an extremely affluent family in Michigan, you wouldn't have had any problem enlisting their support for an important cause. The White man who opened the door probably worked at General Motors and his children attended the University of Michigan and had good summer jobs. Today, try knocking on the same door and he will respond:

"Do you realize my son-in-law has an MBA from Northwestern University and can't get a job in his field?" Hence, he'd be less likely to consider sponsoring a scholarship program for minorities and/or other projects designed to address economic and social disparities. This is what has happened to America. It's divided. It's apathetic. It's been lulled into a lethargic, every-man-and-woman-for-himself mentality.

But these barriers are not impenetrable. Those bent on success simply have to be more self-reliant and creative. I saw a wonderful illustration of this while attending an automotive show in Germany and noticed an SUV with a mirror attached to the driver's side—inside. This was in addition to the standard issue vanity mirror on the passenger side. I was taken aback. When I inquired about the purpose of the extra interior mirror, a representative explained that it allowed drivers to check on children sitting in the back seat. I smiled and asked, "What lady invented that?" The guy laughed. He and I both realized that, although the device was functional, most men would never have thought of it.

That was an opportunity. That was a woman's intuition. That was a woman being a mother. I often refer back to this story when I talk about diversity because it demonstrates how a company —and its bottom line— can benefit from what everyone is bringing to the table. I'm not a gambling man, but I'm willing to bet that several male engineers could have worked on that same SUV but would not have walked out of that design session with the brilliant and groundbreaking idea of a mirror that allowed drivers to keep an eye on their children.

This is evidence of the growing demand for gender-blind opportunities. In the 1950s if you went to New York University or Columbia University or the University of Michigan, you might have found that, among the students enrolled in the master's of business administration, medical, or dental programs, less than 10 percent were White women. If you visited the same schools in 2015, you may have found that 55 percent to 60 percent were White women. What changed? Did White women become smarter or did White men become more enlightened? The opportunities are there, and they were not there before. It's as simple as that. Once the opportunities surfaced, so did the female students. They were already prepared, just like they were in 1950. Yet the system comprised primarily of White men wouldn't give them a chance.

What do you do in a situation like that? What if—due to age, gender, or race—you are being blocked from the circumstances that yield success? Well, this is where I resort to platitudes. Work five times harder. Be better than the best. Believe in yourself. Carve out opportunities where there are no opportunities. And, last but not least, when your big break finally presents itself, make sure you don't make the common mistakes that can chase it away. In other words, don't ruin your chances by committing the following errors:

BRAGGING

If you have this habit and refuse to kick it, you're setting yourself up for rejection after rejection. You'll lose clients and destroy meaningful relationships that could have helped you farther down the road. Believe in yourself, but at the same time, be modest. It's common sense.

GIVING UP TOO SOON

During the California Gold Rush, droves of people went West in search of their fortune. Some of them claimed a plot of land and worked it feverishly for five or six years, but to no avail. Feeling defeated, they sold their plots for about $100, returned home, and found a job in a meat packing plant. Six months later, a few of them received a letter that caused their jaws to drop and their hearts to sink. The person who bought their plot had just struck gold. This is a true scenario and a powerful testament to the importance of never giving up.

HITCHING YOUR WAGON TO THE WRONG DREAM

Don't open a hamburger joint at a monastery for Hindu monks. Okay, this is a far-fetched example, but you get my point. Test the market. Do your due diligence. Also, be authentic to yourself and make sure the opportunity is the right fit. I was once offered a job as Associate Director of the U.S. Small Business Administration in Washington, D.C. I turned it down. The job paid around $100,000 a year, but at the time I was on the fast track with my McDonald's franchises. Meanwhile, another individual who was more politically connected than I was at the time accepted a similar position. Four years later, he resigned and built an impressive company based on contracts from the Department of Defense, the Federal Aviation Administration, and others. He later sold his company for more than $200 million. It's important to note that he was a political operative and a Washington insider. I was neither. I have no regrets about my decision.

FALSE PRIDE

Be willing to start at the bottom. Sure, you have big plans. But along the way, you might have to mop a few floors or flip a few burgers. I did both. In the end, it all paid off. Yet, I know of more than one instance of people who turned down business offers because they didn't want to start on the low rung of the ladder. They kept their sights on executive positions within leading corporations. Sadly, their attempts to start at the top didn't go too well, and their dreams never materialized. The lesson here is simple—a little humility never hurt anyone. In Detroit, there was a 56-year-old man who walked eight hours covering 21 miles to and from work every day because he couldn't afford a car. He did this even in blizzard conditions and below-zero degree weather. Somehow, the local newspaper discovered his situation and sent a reporter out to interview him. The story went viral. Eventually, three GoFundMe pages were started. They raised more than $350,000 and he ended up with a nice, suburban apartment that was closer to his job and a brand-new 2015 Ford Taurus.

I see it like this: There are always opportunities being born and opportunities yet to be made. But you have to push yourself and get involved in making them happen. Lolly Daskal, President and CEO of Lead From Within, explains it this way: "Opportunities are in front of you everyday but to see them you need to look at the world as a place of hope and possibility, not limits, obstacles, and problems."

It's so easy to think: I don't have any money. I don't have any resources. I don't have any of these things I see in *The Wall Street Journal, Town & Country, Vanity Fair, Black Enterprise, Essence,* or on TV. How am I ever going to build a business? But while you're drowning yourself in self-doubt and busily listing all the reasons why you can't do it, there is someone else, worse off than you, who is doing it, even as you read these words. And there's someone who did it long ago when her only hope was a prayer and a bended knee.

In the post-Civil War era, that someone was the daughter of former slaves. At a time when her peers were doing anything they could to survive, she proudly made the declaration: "I don't want to work for no White folks and I don't want to work in nobody's kitchen." They called her Pig Foot Mary, and she was quite a sight—an imposing Black woman who stood on a Harlem street corner from sunup to sundown, selling pig's feet and hog maws out of a beat-up baby carriage. In 1901, Mary, whose real name was Lillian Harris Dean, migrated from Mississippi to New York with nothing but pennies in her pocket and a whole lot of determination in her soul.

Grudgingly, she accepted a job as a domestic, but as soon as she earned a grand total of $5, she bought the baby buggy and loaded it up with her good tasting, down-home foods. There were other folks, just like her, who'd fled to the North in search of a better life. The way Pig Foot Mary saw it, they missed their mama's cooking and it would be real easy to tempt them with the sassy aroma of her hot, smoking chitlins and sizzling corn on the cob.

Her plan worked like a charm. In no time at all, she was able to purchase a steamer and park it near a newsstand across from a local saloon. Plenty of Negroes hung out there and they became her loyal patrons. By 1929 Mary had amassed $375,000, no small task for an illiterate, uneducated Black woman who was raised in a shack. In today's market, that $375,000 would be the equivalent of $5.1 million.

Remember that the next time you ask: Where are the opportunities? Think about the resolve of Pig Foot Mary and then remind yourself: Proactivity is opportunity's accountability partner.

PRINCIPLE THREE: FINANCE

*"A big part of financial freedom is having your heart and
mind free from worry about the what-ifs of life."*
—Suze Orman

Her words rang in my ear and I listened patiently. I didn't
agree with what she was saying, but this was mama speaking and, even in my advanced years, I wasn't about to talk back.

"Boy, you going crazy," she said in her sharpest tone. "You're working too hard. Money can't make you happy."

I gazed at my dear old mother fondly and nodded my head. I never told her what I was thinking that day, but if I had it would have sounded something like this:

"No ma'am, money can't buy happiness, but it's certainly a good down payment."

After I had attained a certain level of wealth, many of my conversations with my mother began and ended that way. She would talk about the evils of money and I would respond with silent respect. I understood the source of her suspicions, and I didn't want to make her think I had strayed from my home training.

For the record, I'm not obsessed with money. It's not that big of a deal to me. But, I do put it up there with oxygen and water. I'm also the first to point out that money is not the root of all evil, as some people believe. On the contrary, the lack of money is the root of all evil. The lack of money can lead to despair, desperation, depression, sickness, and abject poverty.

But while the lack of money is a dream killer, when it's abundant it can be misunderstood, abused, and even feared. Secretly, people see it as the stuff of sorcerers, the nectar of kings and queens. It's shrouded in mystery and wrapped up in ancient folklore. Genies arise from lanterns and hand it to us. Everyday citizens hit the lottery and get rewarded with it. The children of the rich and famous have it bestowed upon them at birth.

Even the Bible references wealth, bringing it up at least 800 times: "The rich rule over the poor, and the borrower is slave to the lender." *(Psalms 22:7)*

So it's no surprise when a would-be entrepreneur gets caught up in the hype. I'm referring to those inexperienced up-and-comers who tend to hesitate or make excuses. If this describes you, then here's a quick question: When the business climate seems inviting and opportunities are rising like a tide over a moonlit sea, why do you freeze?

The answer: You're eager to launch a business, but you can't seem to stop fretting about one key component—seed capital. You're wondering where it is and how you're going to get it. The magical allure of money has you under its spell and you have convinced yourself that you'll never be able to acquire the revenue needed to get your operation off the ground.

You are not alone. The thought of seeking out a loan is

intimidating enough to make the average aspirant drop the notion all together. More often than not, people with great ideas never pursue them because they think of money as an insurmountable hurdle.

Nothing could be further from the truth.

Notice I said the "thought" of securing funds is intimidating. The reality is another story. Financing is actually the easiest aspect of entrepreneurship. Yes, you're reading this correctly. I'm telling you to relax. Funding is as simple as the alphabet and far more accessible than you think.

I know that sounds like an outrageous claim. However, everything is financeable. Most good ideas get financed. And a lot of bad ideas get financed. There's a guy in Michigan who has a reputation for investing in almost anything. Years ago, someone came up with the unusual notion that gas station pumps should include speakers that broadcast advertisements. Most investors found the concept, well, different. The next thing I knew, commercials were airing every time I lifted the lever of a gas pump at a suburban station. You guessed it—the investor (who shall remain unnamed) financed the deal. So you see, all you have to do is be inventive, flexible, and fearless.

Nearly all entrepreneurs start out with no money. Many of them are just as broke as the next person. Yet they achieve their goals anyway. As actor Woody Allen once said, "80 percent of success is just showing up." Or as my grandmother used to explain, "You take one step, and God will take two." Which is another way of saying: Go forth with your business plans and, sooner or later, the money will appear.

With that said, I must warn you that most startups are not

financed by banks. Instead, startups are funded by a host of alternative sources. My situation is an ideal example. The McDonald's opportunity surfaced while I was still working on a Ph.D. at The Ohio State University. My Alpha Phi Alpha fraternity brothers urged me to take out a student loan and I heeded their advice. I have already shared this story, but it bears repeating because it demonstrates how smooth the process can be. You see, that $10,000 loan changed my life and forever altered the way I view finance options.

It was a hefty chunk of cash that helped me get my foot in the door of the world of free enterprise. But here's the memory that makes me want to shout—I didn't have to pay all of the debt. The loan conditions stated that 10 percent would be forgiven every year I worked in a public educational institution. I took a job teaching at Wayne State University in Detroit and when I walked out several years later, almost half of my loan was paid off.

So allow me to reiterate: Finance is the easiest part of the entrepreneurial adventure. Most of us don't come from families that can write us a $1 million check and tell us to get out in the world and make our mark. But, we have at our fingertips a supreme resource called creativity. Numerous studies have shown that children who grow up in families where there was entrepreneurship are more inclined to become entrepreneurs. If you have this advantage, then build upon it. If not, follow the examples set by parents and grandparents, aunts, and uncles who knew how to borrow from Peter to pay Jamal and juggle what little they had left.

How is it that Big Mama always came up with the money to get June Bug out of jail? Figure out how she maneuvered, then do it yourself. In most cases, that means turning to the same sources our ancestors relied on—The Three F's. Do not underestimate these Three F's: Friends, Family, and Fools. When you're starting out, the people in your immediate circle will be your cheering squad and No. 1 financers. Surprisingly, many of them will be far more willing to chip in than you ever imagined. Budding businessmen and women turn to friends and family because they're the people who tend to believe in them when no one else does, and they'll offer whatever assistance they can. And do I have to explain fools? They're those starry-eyed individuals who will dig into their pockets whenever they hear about anything that sounds remotely promising. Either that or they just like to gamble every chance they get. Go ahead, give them that chance.

But there is one "chance" I urge you to avoid at all costs: payday loans. These unregulated loans typically are a minimal amount of money with outrageously high interest rates and they must be paid off by the time you receive your next paycheck. Stay away from payday loans and other bottom feeders that will leave you mired in exorbitant fees and other pitiful consequences.

And while you're at it, don't depend solely on grants. I frequently get asked about grants for entrepreneurs. I used to reply "as soon as I ever find out about a grant, after I get mine, I'm going to call you." Today, a shift has occurred. Some grants and government-assistance programs have recently sprung up. However, your own savings, if you have them, are the primary revenue stream with absolutely no strings attached. Many entrepreneurs draw their initial seed capital from personal bank accounts they have strategically grown over the years. Others do a considerable amount of research and dig up a host of unconventional lending options. They include:

COMMUNITY DEVELOPMENT CORPORATIONS

Just as their title suggests, community development corporations are responsible for community services as well as affordable housing. They will also fund businesses that fit their mission, as long as the business is located within certain ZIP Codes. If the company you're starting is considered an enhancement or service to a designated urban or rural area, a community development corporation may be for you.

THE U.S. SMALL BUSINESS ADMINISTRATION (SBA)

This government agency supports entrepreneurs and small businesses, and also backs small business loans administered through other lenders, such as banks and credit unions. In addition, there are many other federal, state, and local government agencies that provide loans.

CREDIT UNIONS AND ALUMNI ASSOCIATIONS

Credit unions are a good option. One of my first business loans came from a credit union. Your alumni association, or place of worship may have a credit union, as they are usually started by people who work together, pray together, know each other well, or have some other factors in common. Credit unions have shown better repayment rates than traditional banks.

CHURCHES

Places of worship are good loan sources, particularly if you or a relative are longtime members. Many a student has been able to go off to college because Sister Williams or Brother Jackson passed the plate around. A number of churches also have loan departments for trustworthy members who have a viable plan to become independent.

INVESTMENT CLUBS

Typically, these clubs are comprised of individuals who have formed a group to pool their money for investment purposes. However, some investment clubs also make small business loans.

FRATERNITIES AND SORORITIES

When I was an undergrad, I secured a $250 loan from the graduate chapter of my fraternity, Alpha Phi Alpha, to pay for a room in my college dormitory. In addition, the Flint chapter of the NAACP had a credit union. The manager, Edgar G. Holt, agreed to loan me $150 for tuition.

VENTURE CAPITALISTS

They are a great alternative resource. Venture capitalists take a risk on something and invest their money on the concept during its initial stages. While angel investors are individuals, venture capitalists are firms or companies.

ANGEL INVESTORS

Also known as seed investors, angel investors are successful entrepreneurs who provide startup capital in exchange for equity in a business that they believe has great potential. The Reality TV Show, *Shark Tank,* features angel investors who listen to pitches from small business owners.

CROWDFUNDING

Crowdfunding websites such as GoFundMe are increasingly popular. A startup company or an individual in distress sets up an online account to collect funds. Various people donate small amounts until the desired goal has been reached.

FOUNDATIONS

These groups give out loans and grants and have become big players in the entrepreneurship industry. The trick is to think holistically and brainstorm for ways to ensure that your effort meets the concerns of a particular community. Let's say you want to open a barber shop on a street that's pockmarked with dilapidated buildings. Here's what you do: Meet with officials at the nearby university and explain that you'd like to create a barber shop in the area, but it can't happen unless certain structures are demolished. If the university wants to see improvements in the surrounding community (and I assure you, it does) it might write a grant to a specific foundation. Before you know it, your goal has been achieved.

SPECIALTY LOANS

As I write this in 2016, there are a myriad of programs designed to finance businesses run by women and military veterans, or to provide incentives for companies to hire them. For instance, the federal government has been known to offer up to $5,000 to businesses that hire veterans. There are even incentives offered to entrepreneurs to hire people who were formerly incarcerated, or workers laid off for five years or more. There also are tax abatements, interest-free loans, and loan forgiveness for businesses that satisfy some very specific parameters. You can get zero-interest loans if you open your business in a certain ZIP Code where development and revitalization plans are underway.

SOU-SOUS

Certain ethnic groups, such as Nigerians, Koreans, and West Indians, create sou-sous. The concept of the sou-sou—which is said to have originated in West Africa—remains popular among people from the Caribbean. A sou-sou is a savings arrangement where members of the group pool an equal amount of money for a set period of time, ranging from weeks, months, a year, etc. During each rotation, one person gets a "hand," which represents the total, lump sum of group money for that period. The sou-sou keeps doing rotations until everyone in the group has had a turn and has received the full lump sum of his or her hand at least once. It's not unusual for the person who created a given sou-sou to take a "cut" from each hand as a fee in exchange for administering the sou-sou. Some argue that it's easier to just keep saving and achieve the same lump-sum effect, especially if the dealer is taking a cut. However, if you're the second in line to receive a lump sum, and the number of people involved is very large, then you may have the equivalent of thousands or tens of thousands of dollars that could take you years to save on your own. Many people use sou-sous to start businesses, buy homes, invest in property, and make other significant purchases.

SMALL BUSINESS INCENTIVES

Many cities spur development by establishing special programs with small business incentives, such as Invest Atlanta and Invest Detroit. There are programs like this across the United States. Either on your own—or, hopefully, with the help of a hired, seasoned professional—explore all of the different programs that exist in almost every city to help new, inexperienced entrepreneurs. They're out there, but without professional help, you may have to know somebody who knows somebody, and hope you get to the right person.

If you have the money, it's best to hire financial professionals to help you navigate the web of potential funding sources. If you can't afford that right now, then I recommend two do-it-yourself resources—SCORE, the Service Corps of Retired Executives, which provides free small business mentoring advice, and your local public library. If you can find one, a business branch of the library is even better. However, as soon as you have the financial wherewithal to do so, I strongly advise you to hire a professional to whom you can delegate this important and complex task.

After you have exhausted all of your options, keep going. Seek and you shall find. Perhaps your business down payment is just around the corner. If not, maybe it's in your best interest to pull out a larger net and catch a bigger fish, as in an actual bank loan. This is atypical the first time out, but it does happen in certain circumstances. Depending on the scale of the enterprise, a traditional bank loan might be necessary either to launch or expand your business. But as you prepare to move forward, don't lose sight of one important fact—banks are not in business to lose money. Your banker and the bank he or she represents are conservative by nature. If your banker wasn't conservative when hired, then he or she will become conservative very quickly, or that banker won't be employed for long.

Let's look at a loan from the perspective of a bank. All a bank does is take Ms. Jones's money and give her 1 percent or 2 percent interest, and loan you Ms. Jones' money, and then charge you between 7 percent to 10 percent interest. Your repayment of the loan allows the bank to give Ms. Jones back her 1 percent or 2 percent interest, and use the remainder to pay employee salaries and other operating costs, and to turn a profit.

If you plan to go this route, make sure you have a job first. And make sure you keep it long enough to save money and develop a good relationship with the banker. Tell your banker that you're working and want to grow your savings account. Explain that one day you hope to go into business for yourself. A year later, when your banker has seen you consistently saving money every month—even if it's in increments of $30, $50, or $75—and maintaining a credit card debt that is zero or very low, you will have his or her attention. If you're paying off your card balance every month, so you're not paying any interest, not only have you become a regular customer, your banker will also know that you are a good manager of your resources, no matter how limited they are.

Whether you want to borrow $100 or $100 million, the first thing a lending institution will look at is your own financial well being: your credit score, the status of your student loans, the status of your credit card bills, how much credit card debt you have, and your debt-to-income ratio. If that's intact, congratulations! You can now hop on the highway to entrepreneurship.

But, first you'll need a solid business plan. You cannot request a bank loan without one. I tell students that a business plan is the bedrock of any good business, but not to worry if they don't reach their goals immediately. After 120 days, some businesses aren't anywhere near their initial business plans. The important thing is to establish one. I always urge my students to map out a five-year business plan without focusing too much on cash flow. I'm more interested in the plan and the SWOT analysis (Strength, Weaknesses, Opportunities, and Threats).

The plan and the SWOT are critical. And, like the funding, they're not difficult to establish. All business conferences have trained individuals available to assist you with your business plan and help you refine your SWOT analysis. Once completed, you can approach a bank with confidence and a clear understanding of your direction, despite your inexperience.

I know this all too well. When I first took out that student loan to cover my equity stake in our McDonald's franchise, it felt like a breeze. However, the completed transaction still involved a bank loan and personal guarantee on the part of the entrepreneur. The first loan was Small Business Administration-guaranteed, but we had to take out a $100,000 loan to give to McDonald's. We gave the bank $25,000, and the bank had exposure for the remainder. We got a guarantee from the Small Business Administration that they would cover 90 percent of the loan if we defaulted. In our case, that guarantee reduced the bank's liability exposure to less than 10 percent.

Our banker had worked for Small Business Administration, and had secured an SBA-backed loan at 3 percent interest. Those we were dealing with at McDonald's corporate headquarters couldn't believe that we had gotten such a low interest rate.

I'll never forget the day we strolled into the bank—a trio of ambitious, young Black men, all under the age of 30—ready to wheel and deal with the big fellas. We felt invincible. My partner, Ray Snowden, a Ph.D. candidate, had written out an agenda for the meeting. Our banker, Aubrey Lee, was deeply impressed by our level of organization.

When the loan interview ended, Lee said to us, "I'd like to talk to you without your accountant." After our accountant left, he remarked, "You three brothers have a lot of education, but you don't know a damn thing about business. I'm going to give you three things you must do." He then listed the following:

1. Stay in your business. Be there every day.

2. Don't get involved in charitable giving to numerous community organizations right away. You can do that later.

3. For God's sake, don't buy a Cadillac. Get a Chevrolet, drive it, and save your money. I want you to pay this loan back.

We followed his advice to the letter. But my journey into the land of loans was far from over. In between the student loan I had used to cover my share of our McDonald's franchise and this Small Business Administration-backed loan, I also received a small loan from a credit union. For a while, I was what was considered an absentee co-owner of our franchise. Eventually, McDonald's gave me an ultimatum. I was told to be on site full-time or relinquish my stake in the partnership. In order to meet this demand, I had to move from Cleveland to Detroit immediately. The Mount Sinai Federal Credit Union saved the day with a loan for my moving expenses.

I sought out the loan bandwagon again when my partners and I came up with the idea for Vitec Automotive. It was 1997 and we wanted to build a plant that would manufacture plastic fuel tanks, a revolutionary concept at the time. Up until the 1970s, cars had steel bumpers. Back then, the gas tanks used in cars and trucks were also made out of steel. Gas is highly combustible and steel tanks were the only ones considered durable enough to prevent explosions.

But we were focused on newer, more resistant, plastic tanks. They were destined to become a game changer. We believed in them and wanted to be part of the shift that would soon take place within the auto industry. We located a company in Michigan named Walbrough, which had been making plastic gas tanks for lawn mowers and snow blowers. They were interested in moving into making plastic gas tanks for cars and trucks as well. They felt they could transition into this new enterprise more quickly as part of a minority joint venture because they assumed this affiliation would also make them a more attractive supplier to original equipment manufacturers, also called OEMs, such as Ford, Chrysler, and General Motors.

That's when the doors slammed shut. Not a single bank in Detroit wanted to finance the deal. One banker confided in me that the problem was that this deal hit on all four "New P's":

- New Process: Manufacturing plastic fuel tanks.

- New Product: The plastic fuel tanks themselves.

- New Plant: We needed to build an entirely new facility to manufacture the fuel tanks.

- New People: This was code for the fact that Black folks would be the primary employees.

In order to be an attractive loan candidate, we should not have had more than two of the four P's. But we refused to give up. Our attorney connected with a Chicago-based financial broker and made him part of our team. This guy was a dynamo who shopped our plastics concept all over the country.

We got six offers and ended up going with Bank of America out of Chicago.

Think about it: Same deal, same location, same people on our team, but because we hired this finance guy who knew the full breadth of our options, we were able to get it done. The moral of this story is that there is no sense sitting around moaning and groaning about what you cannot do. While you're complaining that you can't make it work, someone else has caught the ball and carried it to the finish line. As an entrepreneur, you have to make it happen. You have to try. You have to keep going. Persistence is its own form of capital when it comes to seeking and obtaining financing.

Here's some real talk:

- Start small, learn, lose, go down, get back up, and learn some more. In the corporate world, there is the concept of the tone at the top. The CEO and other members of the C-Suite that drives management create a company's culture, values, and work ethic. When we started Vitec, I was the primary shareholder. Therefore, I stayed off payroll for three years. In doing so, I was sending a message to our team that if I'm not getting paid, we must manage this company like we're all here running on empty.

- Ignore old-school advice that's preventing you from experiencing a new-school paradigm. Only a few years ago Black folks would say, "Don't you quit that good job to go into no business." Similarly, young people who had just graduated from college and were starting their career would hear, "Why don't you get a steady job? That's what you went to school for. And, for God's sake, don't quit and go chasing some foolish pipe dream."

- It's okay to resign from your daily nine-to-five hustle, but please pace yourself. Don't suddenly quit your job just because you heard about a new pizza franchise coming to town. Start stashing away money now, read, do your due diligence, network, build relationships, and work or volunteer in the kind of business you want to own.

- Finance is an ongoing process. As I mentioned earlier, once you secure it, you're not home-free. You have to make sacrifices and one of those sacrifices often translates into no salary for awhile. This act communicates nonverbally to the entire C-Suite and all the managers in your firm: *I want to see your expense report. I want to see every penny that goes out of this business.* I stayed off the payroll for several years for every new company that I started. Fortunately, every time I've done so, these ventures have worked out.

- Pay off debts and don't over-invest. As an investor, I'm cautious. I don't invest in things that I don't understand, and I don't invest more money than I can afford to lose. I don't own any bonds, and I've predominantly parked my investments in certificates of deposit (CDs) which pay me around 1 percent interest. Some may think that's nuts for someone of my net worth. A typical financial advisor will wag a finger at that. At 1 percent, those CDs are failing to outpace inflation. However, I try to keep my personal, long-term debt at zero or below.

- Attend business conferences and seminars. Whenever people are talking business you should be there, networking and forming relationships. After all, this is your dream. You have to nurture it to bring it to life.

- Donate, donate, donate! The money you donate not only helps others, it comes back to you. I am a cheerful giver. I give away more than half-a-million dollars every year to educational and charitable organizations and nonprofits, with a special emphasis on Black organizations. This reflects my values.

- Reek with conservatism. This means your briefcase, your clothing, and your car. If necessary, drive your neighbor's car, but do not arrive at a bank, agency, credit union, or any other potential loan office in your BMW, wearing a $9,000 suit, dripping in jewelry, and toting a Gucci handbag. Don't flaunt accessories that represent symbolic wealth. Represent a lifestyle of reasonableness. Whether you're a billionaire or a thousandaire, a lifestyle of reasonableness through your physical appearance conveys to your banker your reasonableness with your resources. It helps your banker to understand that you're a good money manager. If you're flashy, your banker will think: *You've got your loan on. You don't need one from me.*

- Stay away from social media broadcasts that have the potential to put your career in jeopardy. By now, I'm sure you've heard horror stories about people losing jobs because of something posted on social media, usually Twitter or Facebook, that embarrasses their company. This conflict occurs at all levels, from waitresses who have made racist comments or badmouthed their employer to corporate vice presidents who have plastered remarks on social media that conflict with the corporation's values. It's common knowledge that companies check Facebook pages before making job offers. What would stop an institution from doing the same thing when it's considering you for a loan?

- Savings is the name of the game. The simple act of saving, as my dear friend Ray Snowden taught me, is one of the keys to creating the collateral necessary to secure loans and build wealth. Other keys are consistency in the form of saving consistently or constantly keeping track of your spending, discipline, balance, and being able to distinguish between wants and needs.

- Use your wealth to set a positive financial tone for your family and community. In the Bible it states, "A good man leaves an inheritance to his children's children." *(Proverbs 13:22)* Aim for wealth that is transferrable and intergenerational. After a head-of-household dies, the family has to cope with a funeral and the burden of grief. When entrepreneurs don't carefully plan with their accountants and lawyers, especially estate lawyers, on all matters concerning their wills and estate, the impact is even more devastating.

Since I'm pretty sure you'll get overwhelmed at some point, I'd like to remind you of the old adage: "A fool and his money are soon parted." Think about the numerous entertainers, athletes, and lottery winners who attained wealth and lost it because they didn't follow a few ground rules and learn how to invest. That should light a fire under you for a while and keep you focused.

Black folks aren't broke, but traditionally, some of us have made bad choices. I'd like to remind you once again that wealthy people teach their children to acquire; middle income people teach their children to sell, and poor people teach their children to consume. It's time to break this cycle. Be the role model, the family member who is successful in securing seed capital for one initial venture, and then continues to build upon it for the rest of his or her life.

Most of my current net worth is not from McDonald's by a long shot. However, that's where it was born. Everything I have today originated from that first franchise deal. It was thanks to earnings from the various McDonald's restaurants that we owned that I had $150,000 in savings to provide the collateral

I needed to then get a $150,000 loan to buy Regal Plastics, a company I acquired much later. That initial loan led to more and more.

But I wouldn't have eked out the maximum benefits of that entry-level financing experience if I hadn't developed a lifelong habit of being disciplined, penny-wise, and practical. Everybody in my family knows that my first inclination is not to spend money. I'm a generous brother, but I can be tight as a fist. Generally, I don't buy what I don't need. That makes me the frugal one in my group. I have friends who drive Bentleys and wear $5,000 worth of clothing every day. I can afford to live that way, but that's not how I roll. I'm content with a good book and a nice sweater.

I also avoid the *Four C's*:

- **Car:** My grandad always said, "It's OK to own a Cadillac, but you need to park it every night on some land that you own." I've also heard it said, "If you have a Land Ranger and a Land Rover and also have a landlord, you are a landless fool."

- **Clothes:** I once read that Black men buy 80 percent of all the shoes in America that cost more than $400. Recently, I noticed that a major sneaker manufacturer was making a special line for Black History Month that cost $240 a pair. We must walk, but do we need to walk like that? And for all the ladies with those designer purses: What sense does it make to walk around with a $9,000 bag when you don't even have $900 in the bank?

- **Cosmetics:** Black people are 13 percent of the population, but Black women buy 30 percent of cosmetics in America, and many of them pay for those items with a credit card.

- **Credit card:** There's such a thing as "good" debt—think student loans, small-business loans, or mortgages. Abusing department store credit cards, frivolously living beyond your means, and fulfilling wants via credit cards does not qualify as "good" debt—or as good anything.

The *Four Cs* are the traps created by a pesky little habit I call retail therapy. Often, people who feel powerless try to validate themselves with expensive things they can't afford. I don't fault them for wanting to pull themselves up. I just wish they would realize the road to wealth is not paved with debt. One of my business partners and I learned that the hard way. Frankly, it was a lesson for all of us. When we opened our third franchise, I wasn't as financially savvy as I am now, and none of us was the best steward of money. We were young, inexperienced, and had no idea that folks who shell out seed capital often know more about you than you know about yourself.

One day, a helicopter mysteriously appeared over a home one of my partners was building in a ritzy Michigan suburb. As it turned out, it was transporting a couple of "spy" executives from the corporate office of an institution that was considering him for a loan. The problem was that he was spending money on new property at a time when he was already knee deep in debt. His request was swiftly denied.

Don't think you can hide missed bill payments. You can't. Don't assume you can mask your credit woes either. When it comes to your financial history, your potential lenders are several steps ahead of you. If there are lingering debts, simply come clean and explain what happened —you were laid off from your job, a parent was sick, etc. Honesty is the best policy in all endeavors, especially when establishing a reputation as an entrepreneur. Everything you do —every false move and every good one, every major personal purchase and every business acquisition —will be weighed.

Again, I've been there. Almost as soon as I became a managing partner of Detroit's MGM Grand Casino, I received a phone call and, of course, I was expecting it. It was from my sweet, but overprotective, mother. She had just finished reading a newspaper article about my new venture and, boy, was she upset. The idea of her son being affiliated with a casino didn't rest well with her.

"Bill, don't do it," she warned. "That's tainted money."

I smiled. But this time I mustered up a response.

"Don't worry, Ma' Dear," I said. "The only time money is tainted is when there tain't enough of it."

PRINCIPLE FOUR: RELATIONSHIPS

"Lots of people want to ride with you in the limo,
but who you want is someone who will take the bus with
you when the limo breaks down."
—Oprah

Whenever a deal is about to collapse, I turn to a guy known for his quick thinking and unorthodox theories. I call him Larry "Out-of-the-Box" Crawford. He's a Detroit area dentist-turned-entrepreneur whose investment ideas are so unusual they often defy reason.

He's also one of the most respected members of my squad.

My squad—Larry Crawford, Ron Hall, Alex Parrish, Dennis Archer, Roy Roberts, Don Snider, Ray Snowden, Gordon Follmer, Thomas Dortch Jr., and Roosevelt Adams—consists of close friends with whom I share interests, values, and goals. I call them my squad, but we're actually more like a tribe in a communal village. We have a strong bond and a life-long loyalty. We have depended upon one another, rescued one another and taught one another a thing or two about etiquette, history, ethics, and business.

My understanding of the luxury car industry? I got that from Hall. Politics? That's from the former Mayor Archer, of course. Snider and Crawford showed me how to network. Snowden taught me to save. Follmer inspired me to believe there's a solution to every problem. Adams, Dortch, Roberts and Parrish? They're natural diplomats who helped me to expand my vision and grow as a civic leader.

Good relationships are like that. When they are carefully nurtured and cultivated, they can be more valuable than your weight in diamonds. In many ways, a trusted comrade is like having access to a secret code. He or she can magically open doors. Here's why: The people you kick it with today —that gangly brother on the basketball court or your homeboys from the dorm —could be part of your network, alliance, or political connections tomorrow. They could be your future references, referral sources, and business leads. They are the special path that you have already paved.

Just look at it this way: Let's say you have a degree in marketing and your college roommate works in the human resources department at a Fortune 500 company. If you need a job, who are you going to call? Then there's your former biology lab partner. Pretend, for a minute, that he's now part owner of a fabulous, five-star hotel. What if I told you that you'd get cool points and your business worth would increase exponentially every time you and this brother were seen together?

Not convinced? Well, let me break it down further.

There was once a rich investor in New York who I'll call Joseph Thompson (not his real name). During the Great Depression, he lost everything. So he decided to reach out to his friend, John D. Rockefeller. Because he had fallen so low on the social totem pole, Thompson was kind of worried that, perhaps, Rockefeller wouldn't bother to take his call. He phoned his office anyway and told his secretary that he wanted to invite Rockefeller out to lunch.

Rockefeller accepted and agreed to meet with Thompson the following day. As the two strolled down Wall Street to his private club, heads turned and people began to whisper: *"That's Joseph Thompson with John D. Rockefeller, but isn't Thompson flat broke? I don't know, that's Rockefeller with him. Rockefeller always knows what's going on."*

Both men entered the club and Rockefeller was shown to his private table. The buzz continued among those gathered. Immediately, Rockefeller excused himself to go wash his hands. At that moment, several people of wealth and influence approached Thompson and began showering him with requests to meet to discuss potential business deals. When Rockefeller returned and asked Thompson what he wanted to talk about, all Thompson could do was smile.

"Don't worry," he said. "I have it all taken care of."

We've all heard of guilt by association. Well this was a case of success by association. When the other club members saw Thompson with Rockefeller they automatically assumed that he was someone worth getting to know. This has often been referred to as "birds of a feather flock together," which is one of the oldest and most common expressions ever uttered. It's also one of the truest. We are judged by the company we keep, in good ways and not so good ways.

During my early high school years of goofing off and thinking little of myself, I stuck with the crowd of underachievers that fit my low self image. And doesn't everyone?

What straight-A students do you know who perpetually hang around with kids who are failing or getting into fights after class? Successful students know that if they set foot on that crooked path, before long they'll be on a fast train to nowhere. I often tell young people that if you see nine broke brothers on a corner, don't join them. If you do, there will be 10 broke brothers. Believe me, if you tell me who your five closest friends are, I can tell you where you're going to be in five to 10 years. Your relationships shape you, define you, and help carve out your future.

How do you find and develop the best relationships? There are at least three approaches:

GET TO KNOW PEOPLE WHO SHARE YOUR VALUES

There are the people who will become your closest friends, your road dogs, those special buddies who remain in your life forever. Sometimes you encounter them in childhood or high school. For me, it was college. I had a terrific roommate named Dennis Archer and we connected like blood brothers. By then, I was no longer the insecure guy who ate lunch under the stairwell and grumbled about school. So, of course, I gravitated to those who shared my newfound interests. Dennis and I both loved books, deep conversations and —well, how can I put this? We also had the same budget, which was no budget at all. We were poor dudes in a dorm that didn't serve food. A lasting bond was formed as we ate Spam, sardines, and potted meat together. Obviously, those were the days. Because of them, Dennis and I have a priceless, lifelong camaraderie. Neither of us had any idea that he would one day become the mayor of Detroit.

CREATE A DOMINO EFFECT

As you and your friends mature, you will begin to make referrals for one another and offer leads to jobs. Possibly, these leads will have a cumulative effect. One friend in a good position will hire another then another. Along the way, the squad will begin to swap investment ideas and/or make plans to pursue a business partnership. Just like tipping dominos, you will push one another forward. If I hadn't had a significant relationship with Detroit Urban League President, Francis A. Kornegay, my meeting with Henry Ford might not have taken place. Kornegay, my longtime mentor, took me to Henry Ford and said, "Henry, this is my boy. He has a bunch of those McDonald's stands, and he wants to be a car dealer." This meeting with Ford was a life-changing experience that led to my ownership of Regal Plastics.

GET IN THE MIX

Being part of the mix is essential because it puts you where you need to be to meet those people you want to know. You have to belong to something, be it a sorority, fraternity, alumni organization, church, community group, or a nonprofit. Get involved. Volunteer. Everyone has a skill and/or an activity they enjoy. Figure out what that activity is for you. But before you do, make sure you know how to pace yourself and manage your expectations. When you volunteer for political campaigns, don't expect to become a director the first time around. Stay humble, and focused on serving. That's the real reason you're there. (Of course, getting in the mix is part of it too, but service always comes first.) Please remember this: There's no mixing without giving, sharing, and doing your best. Pass out flyers, knock on doors, do grunt work. If you're introverted, accept assignments that don't require face-to-face interaction, like making phone calls and reading from a script. Or you can volunteer to do research. In short, when you volunteer for campaigns, or for anything, find the right fit, and be driven by passion without expecting glory. Along the way, something good is bound to happen, often when you're not anticipating it. This is one of the things that fuel my own passion for volunteerism. After I throw myself wholeheartedly into an important cause, someone will suddenly give me a much-needed push or surprise me by opening a door that advances my career.

My current team of confidantes is a direct result of the relationships and networks I deliberately nourished. As I slowly climbed the ladder to success, I met some incredible people who have helped spirit me toward my goals. They are the people I believe in and the people who believe in me. But that type of camaraderie doesn't bloom overnight. An overnight or fly-by-night connection is simply an acquaintance, someone you speak to on campus, make small talk with about the game and/or have friendly, often pleasant, surface relationships. The long term, genuine bonds are the ones you forge over a period of time with individuals with whom you have a more personal connection. You can share information, secrets, dreams, and even money.

A billionaire friend of mine once put it his way: "Who would you give or loan a couple thousand dollars? That's your core guy." If there is someone you wouldn't hesitate to hand a sizeable amount of money, you have exited the realm of acquaintance and entered the territory of dear friend. I call friends who fit in this category my squad. This is the tightest circle imaginable, the brothers with whom you share light-hearted moments, conduct business, and discuss situations and details that you would be embarrassed to share with anyone else.

Within the squad, you can feel vulnerable. While interacting with them, you can let down defensive barriers and peel off whatever mask you might be wearing. Each of them is "a brother from another mother" and each helps you embrace and maximize your potential. But make no mistake, all of our relationships are distinct and a few are fairly complex. Some are friendships coupled with mentorships while others are mentorships and/or friendships combined with sponsorships. Or they are vertical relationships. Regardless, they all comprise the next level up in relationships.

Vertical Relationships are friendships with people who are older, wiser, and more experienced. They are often mentors who take you under their wings and show you the ropes. When developing relationships, especially vertical ones in which people are more advanced in age or their careers than you are, make sure to acknowledge and show appreciation for their assistance. It makes most people feel good to know they are helping others. However, exercise good judgment. Cultivating this feeling in others isn't an open-access pass to becoming needy or greedy.

Mentorships can take different forms, from verbal encouragement and career guidance to lending financial assistance and helping you improve your diction and professional appearance.

Sponsorships are about leverage. A sponsor picks up the phone on your behalf or goes to bat for you on matters and in ways that are critical to your advancement. As a person of influence, a sponsor may put in a word on your behalf that makes the difference between your admission into a master's program at Columbia University—or not. Once you're accepted, unbeknownst to you, that same sponsor may create a $5,000 scholarship that will help defray tuition costs your first year. A sponsor's role is action-oriented.

It's important to note that sometimes your mentor and sponsor have to be two different people. Oftentimes, the person who mentors you doesn't have the capacity or influence to act as sponsor. Two of my favorite professors were Albert Rogers and James Randall. They guided and pushed me through community college. Francis Kornegay (via Henry Ford) opened the door to my highly-profitable entrée into the automotive industry. Dennis Archer included my name in a list of recommendations he gave to MGM Resorts International as possible casino partners in Detroit. At this point my friend, Dennis, became my sponsor as well.

Sponsorship has played a role in my ownership of more than one company. So has networking. Early on in my career, I was on the equivalent of what felt like 99 different boards. I was a single man, and I didn't want to be poor all my life. I willingly signed up for whatever I thought would help me move forward. While on a board for Oakwood Hospital in Michigan, I met John Sagan, someone I would meet again when we went to see Henry Ford II with Dr. Kornegay. Based on our work together on the board, Sagan was able to offer Ford a firsthand assessment of my character. That incident was the perfect cocktail of relationships and politics blended together, yielding wonderful results.

Back in the day, I used to know a big time numbers man who was even more successful than my Uncle Paul. He encouraged me and a dentist friend, Larry (the one I call "Out-of-the-Box" Crawford) to invest in a plastics company in Saginaw. However, General Motors wouldn't do the deal with my buddy, since they didn't know him and he hadn't been in the plastics industry long enough. On the other hand, I was known. My master networking skills paid off and I acquired majority ownership in the firm. Later, I was able to make Crawford a Vitec shareholder and appoint him to the board.

This is a perfect example of the unpredictable, yet highly fruitful, manner in which relationships can work. It's a symphony of give-and-take based on your ability to follow three steps:

A. Network.

B. Network.

C. Repeat steps A and B.

And to all you naysayers who might be reading and furrowing your brow, hear this: I feel you. I know you've heard some unsavory gossip about the networking circuit. I get it. You think it's brown-nosing. You actually believe that getting to know specific people and mingling in certain circles makes you a sellout. You may even be tossing around terms like "waste of time" or "phony." Well, listen up: Nothing could be more off base. You're delusional and it's time to pull your head out of the sand. There is a golden rule and a rock hard truth about success: You either network – or you don't work!

So if you didn't get it the first time, I'll say it again: When you get along great with someone and you really like him or her, that's your friend. However, it just so happens that three years later that same friend might end up at Spelman College or Morehouse College, and become president of the student body. He or she then discovers that the college is developing a program for people from urban areas who are entering college in their 20s. Your friend thinks about you. You apply—and get in. You had simply developed a relationship with a person who was going to college although you hadn't thought that far ahead. That relationship bore fruit in an unexpected and wonderful way.

Understand that I'm not suggesting that you enter relationships thinking this person is going to get you what you need. For instance, a friend of mine once told me about a strange encounter she observed during a vacation in Egypt. One of her traveling companions casually mentioned to the others in their tour group that he hoped to make friends with one of the local citizens. He reasoned that if he made a friend, he wouldn't have to pay for a hotel the next time he traveled to the region. The next day, as they were sitting in a restaurant enjoying dinner, an Egyptian gentleman approached the group and welcomed them to his homeland.

My friend said she watched in horror as her traveling companion introduced himself then immediately asked the man he had just met if he could stay at his home during future visits. This scene is a nightmarish demonstration of brown-nosing at its worst. This is *not*, I repeat, *not* networking. It's a crude example of the stereotypical Ugly American. It also contradicts my message. Do not confuse networking with being a grabby opportunist. That's the complete opposite of what I'm saying here. In fact, that kind of attitude won't get you anywhere.

True networking requires you to shift your mental gears. It means you are befriending someone who brings out the best in you. It suggests that, if needed, you are willing to extend yourself on this person's behalf and follow one of self-help author Dale Carnegie's chief guidelines: "The only way on Earth to influence the other fellow is to talk about what he wants and show him how to get it."

Now that's networking at its peak. But it won't occur unless both individuals click. And it won't flow unless both of you remain principled and authentic. When that type of beautiful synergy is present, it's possible for events to unfold organically. There's an African proverb that states: "If you want to go fast, go alone. If you want to go far, go with others."

Networking means you're inviting others along for the ride. Because I know it's necessary, I learned to do this as best as I could. In fact, I became pretty good at it. I only wish my close friend, the late Ray Snowden, had become as much of a political animal as I had. Ray thought he'd be awarded more McDonald's franchises because he had an incredible work ethic and ran a tight operation at his other franchises. His expectations never materialized. Mine did.

The only differences between us were the genuine relationships I cultivated with those at McDonald's who were influencers and decision-makers in the franchise process. Unlike many people, my political acumen came naturally. In college, I was elected to serve on the Inter-Fraternity Council which consisted of all 15 fraternities on campus—13 White fraternities and the only two Black ones, the Alphas and the Kappas. I recognized early on that if I could get the support of six of the White fraternities and of the two Black fraternities (the latter I had in the bag), I could get anything on my agenda passed. That was my first big experience in navigating the political aspects of life—and I nailed it. Ditto for my daughter, who became president of her senior class at Spelman College with very little effort.

I asked her, "Mary, why did you run for president? You're not from Atlanta, and you're not in a sorority."

She replied, "Dad, I just knew there were only about 300 women I needed to impact in order to win because most of them don't vote."

I responded, "You had 300 names?"

"No," she said. "But I had about 40 people that I knew could impact people." That's how she got her 300.

As I listened to my daughter, I smiled just a bit and fought back a desire to laugh. I recognized myself in my child. I realized then and there that she has both the IQ and EQ (emotional quotient) to navigate relationships and hone political instincts. At an early stage in life, she knows that if she has supporters, she can't fail—at least not completely. Like anything else, there will be speed bumps, challenges, and plenty of questions. Some of the questions I've been asked include:

How Can You Ensure That Certain People Benefit From Your Business Concerns?

That's easy. One of my fondest memories involves another one of my longtime mentors, Art Johnson. Art dedicated his life to public service and spent his 30 years working for the Detroit

NAACP. He focused more on community efforts and public service rather than personal advancement. He was the "Pied Piper" for the NAACP and got me to leave the Urban League to work for them. When I went to work for the Cleveland NAACP, I could call him for advice, which made people think I was smart. Art was 60 years old when I became a co-managing partner in Detroit's MGM Grand. We were able to make him part of the deal.

Is It Okay To Enter A Business Relationship With Someone You Don't Like Personally?

Yes and No. There are people that you may not like but, for pragmatic reasons, you might have to collaborate with them on a business deal. Generally, this doesn't bother me. However—and this is important—there are some people I would never do business with because of their severe and proven moral and ethical deficits.

How Do You Avoid Relationships That Compromise Your Integrity?

There's one incident in my entrepreneurial career that answers this question perfectly. I received a call from a regional vice president of McDonald's who told me the corporation was going to reward me with a franchise within a major business district. This deal was going to be a game changer. As I envisioned the nonstop business that would flow through this new site, I thought to myself: *"This thing is going to print money."* Later, one of the district's executives called and asked to meet. We met at a restaurant in my lawyer's office building. During our meeting, he began to toss around the word partnership. Finally, I asked him flat out if he was asking for a kickback. He acknowledged that he was. I immediately drew our meeting to a close and told him that I didn't want to speak with him anymore. What he was proposing was illegal and went against my business ethics. I had no intention of putting the gaming license that allowed me to be a partner of the MGM Grand Detroit in jeopardy. However, these people would not go away. They approached me several more times, and even my attorney could not get them to be reasonable. They insisted that I "play ball" in order to get the restaurant. Finally, I told them to "take the restaurant and go to hell." Next, I had to tell McDonald's that I couldn't accept the new franchise, but I had to couch it in a way that would not make them think I had lost interest. I explained that my circumstances prohibited a new business endeavor. I said I was newly-married and my mother-in-law had moved into the home I shared with my wife. All of this was true, but not the reason why I stepped away. That restaurant did $5 million in sales its first year at a time when the average McDonald's restaurant was earning $2 million annually. But the executive behind that unsavory scheme was eventually fired.

Is It Possible To Get Business Ideas And Deals From A Passing Acquaintance?

Yes! When I was about 26 years old, I managed to get one of those $99 student deals to Freeport, Bahamas. While I was on the beach, I met a teacher named C.A. Smith who was around 31 years old at the time. We struck up a friendship and stayed in touch. I would see him every other winter or summer. By the time I was appointed by President Ronald Reagan to serve as chairman of the African Development Foundation, C.A. Smith had risen to be a Member of Parliament in the Bahamas. When the Bahamians were trying to craft a deal on the Caribbean Basin Initiative, I was able to lend a hand. Later, C.A. became the Bahamian ambassador to the United States, under the first President Bush. I had an appointment under Bush and was able to help C.A. on some of his initiatives and he was able to reciprocate and help me with some of mine.

Can A Relationship Save You From Disaster?

Absolutely! I had grown Regal Plastics' revenue from $25 million to $50 million, then suddenly the company hit a brick wall. I didn't have the people or resources I needed to keep business flowing, and the bank demanded that I do a personal guarantee or they were going to call in the loan and put the company into bankruptcy. This was one of the worst episodes of my entrepreneurial career. However, my friends were working feverishly to help me save my business. Art Johnson played the conciliator and, with the help of Ron Hall and my attorney, Alex Parrish, we were able to block that worst-case scenario. They convinced the bank to give me more time to stabilize Regal.

Not everyone agrees with me, I'm sure, but I fervently believe in divine order. Fortunately, I have the right squad in place to help things along as well. When I was in my 20s and 30s, whenever I had problems, I would retreat to Ann Arbor, Michigan, and sit in front of the house I had once lived in as a graduate student. I found that setting very meditative. Being there helped me clear my head and reach important decisions. One Friday night, I came home from working late at McDonald's and my place in Detroit was in chaos. The police had conducted a drug raid in the wee hours of the morning that led to a fire in the building. The fire department extinguished the blaze, causing a flood in my apartment. It was a wild night. I immediately headed to the steps of my Ann Arbor refuge.

I lived two minutes away from Interstate 94, which is the straight route that I normally took to get to Ann Arbor. I was going to take my typical drive, get a hot dog along the way, ride around campus, sit in front of my old house, and think. But for some reason, I suddenly decided to take the scenic route down Michigan Avenue.

At that time, Black folks didn't live in that area, known as Dearborn, Michigan. But given what I'd just experienced at my apartment, I wasn't thinking about demographics. I simply pulled up to Michigan and Rotunda Drive and saw a sign that said: *Opening. New Apartments and Townhouses, Fairlane East.* I made a snap decision to stop in and grab a brochure. After that, I headed to Ann Arbor and bought my hot dog. By then it was around 1 p.m. and, although I had been up all night, I had to be back to McDonald's by 5 p.m. for that evening's shift.

As I drove along, I decided to make one last stop, this time to see a friend who lived in the area. After stepping inside her house, I abruptly announced, "I'm fed up. I'm ready to move."

"Move where?" she asked.

I gave her the brochure. She started laughing and said, "This is Dearborn!"

I said, "Dearborn?" I hadn't even thought about the location. It was 1981, and the place I was interested in renting was a three-bedroom unit that would cost me $1,100 a month. That was a sizable amount of money at that time, but I could afford it. It was a very nice area, a quiet, gated community, equipped with a 24-hour security guard.

The Monday after that, I filled out the forms for the apartment, I received an odd phone call from a man I had never met. He told me his name was Larry Washington.

"We see that you filled out an application last Friday," he said.

"Mr. Washington," I said. "I don't know you, but I'm not looking for any trouble. I'm not trying to move into Dearborn."

"Calm down," he responded. "We want this place integrated. I've done my research on you, and you used to work for the NAACP in Cleveland."

"Yes, sir," I answered.

He said, "I'm chairman of the NACCP in Detroit and I want to come by McDonald's in Detroit and talk to you."

When we met in person, he handed me his card. I stared in disbelief. Stamped on the card were the words: *Assistant to Henry Ford II, Chairman and CEO.* (Bear in mind, this all occurred before my meeting with Ford.) Washington added, "All I want you to do is listen to me. You're in the Republican Party—you're Vice Chairman in Michigan. If you agree to move to Dearborn, I will put you on the Oakwood Hospital board, and I will put you on any commission or board you want in the city of Dearborn."

Many of Ford Motor Company's top executives sat on the Oakwood Hospital board. Guess what? I moved to Dearborn.

This sums up the power of reciprocal relationships and the importance of having a network—particularly one of high caliber. Whenever I read about accomplished individuals, I can't help but notice that many of them aligned themselves with like-minded people, all of whom entertained innovative concepts and ideals. These carefully guarded relationships helped those individuals climb to greater heights.

Thomas Edison traveled the world and consorted with his squad—Harvey Firestone, Henry Ford, and Luther Burbank—in order to maximize his talent. Edison was blessed that he had Firestone, Ford, Burbank and others who could challenge him and encourage him to widen his intellectual gifts.

Try it and you'll see what I mean. Gather a group of your most determined friends and set collective and/or individual goals. Then challenge one another to reach them. Years ago, three Black teens from a crime-ridden community in Newark, New Jersey, did that and more. They made a passionate vow to assist one another in their quest to get out of the hood and make their dreams of becoming doctors a reality. These days, they are known as Dr. George Jenkins, Dr. Sampson Davis, and Dr. Rameck Hunt—a dentist and two physicians who readily acknowledge that they were "drawn together for a purpose." Authors of *The New York Times* bestseller, *The PACT*, they now create opportunities for others through their nonprofit, The Three Doctors Foundation. They're also on the lecture circuit, visiting schools across the country and speaking about the experiences that gave birth to their careers.

And how about you? Can you and your crew stick together and make the same quantum leap? Maintaining relationships is easier than you think. Just be willing to take the time. I keep in touch via phone calls, emails, and text messages. I'm also a prolific reader and pass on—unprompted —information I think people will find valuable. Based on their interests, their current life stage, or significant events that have occurred in their lives, I email links to online articles or a heads-up about an upcoming deal or event.

I do this because I cherish the bonds I have formed. No matter what stage of life I enter or how much money I have amassed, I'm still awed and humbled by all the love and support my relationships have provided. And I find that I'm still reaping rewards. My connections have helped maintain my reputation. They keep my pride, my honor, and my word alive. Because my network has my back, my businesses have been able to glide into soft landings at times when I thought they would crash. Enterprises that I never anticipated have soared beyond my wildest hopes. Struggles that could have ruined me financially have morphed into stories of grandeur and triumph.

And I owe it all to my squad.

PRINCIPLE FIVE: TALENT AND SKILL SET

"Talent wins games, but teamwork and intelligence win championships."
—Michael Jordan

There's an old saying about the automobile industry: "Never buy a car that was made on Monday morning."

This idea isn't based on hard evidence. It's simply an insinuation that cars assembled at the beginning of the work week just might be the product of a crew that's recovering from a long weekend of drinking and partying. I don't like generalizing and I prefer not to toss people or situations into stereotypical categories. But, as an entrepreneur who depends on quality labor — both skilled and unskilled—I can't deny that there might be a kernel of truth in the Monday morning theory. In my position, it's certainly something I have to think about. And if you plan to manage employees, it's something you're going to have to think about as well.

You'll find yourself wondering if Pookie, Joe, and Ray-Ray will come to work every day. You'll find yourself pondering why the production output is lower on Fridays. You'll find yourself constantly assessing and reassessing whether or not you have the right staff. At a certain point, you'll even have to face something that no one who takes pride in their own abilities wants to admit: Your talent is only as good as the talent demonstrated by members of your team.

This is not a subject for debate. It's a fact. Chief Executive Officers can't afford to be naïve about the employees they hire or the contractors that provide the services they outsource. These individuals and entities are key to a successful operation. Not only are they responsible for production, they are often the first or last line of defense between you and your patrons. They are your company's image, attitude and voice.

In essence, they fall into three categories – Finders, Minders, and Grinders:

- **Finders:** A Finder is someone charged with business development. This is the person who is out actively identifying prospective new deals, whether it's at the local Chamber of Commerce, the Black Chamber of Commerce, the Young Republicans Club, country and golf clubs, alumni associations, or anywhere potential dealmakers—and deals— might be present. The Finder schedules meetings and goes out every night hunting for deals. Ideally, once a Finder identifies a deal, he or she has a team in place that can turn it over to a Minder.

- **Minders:** Those in C-Suite roles, management or operations, are the Minders: CEO, CFO, CMO, CTO, the chief talent acquisition person, and others, many of whom have MBAs or legal degrees. The Minders work together collaboratively to evaluate and manage a newly identified opportunity and determine whether or not it should evolve into a business deal.

- **Grinders:** Grinders are manufacturing or support staff tasked, ideally, with working together in a positive, collaborative environment to produce products and services.

The success of any business depends on these three interconnected roles. If they aren't fulfilled properly, you can forget about your impeccable credentials or your impressive work ethic. No matter how accomplished you are or how good you might be at your craft, it's the people who work for you and with you who will have lasting impact. There is one exception, however. It's a typical phenomenon that occurs during those lean startup years when the founder and CEO of the establishment has the honor of wearing all three hats. At the infancy stage of your enterprise, you're the taskmaster. You get to do it all.

If that sounds daunting, don't worry. You won't be the first to fly solo. When Dan Price launched Gravity Payments, a credit card processing service, he was a 19-year-old college student working alone in his dorm room. Another young man, Todd Pedersen—best known for Vivent, a home automation service provider—once had the lonely task of running a door-to-door pest control company from a tiny trailer. And during the early 1960s, it wasn't unusual for a certain starry-eyed young songwriter to be up all night, juggling responsibilities for his fledgling recording business. His name was Berry Gordy and the company was Motown Record Corp.

Driven by passion and pride, Gordy had borrowed close to $1,000 from his family loan fund and set out to leave his thumbprint on the world of music. He was the finder who scouted out the talent and sought funding. He was the minder who signed the talent, cut the deals, established a business plan. He was the grinder who wrote new material for his teenage artists and shaped their careers—all on the first floor of his home on Detroit's West Grand Blvd.

No matter what age you are, you probably know the rest of this story by heart. Gordy's brainchild exploded into a national label recognized all over the world. But along with his success, came the growing pains of entrusting his dream to that sea of friends, acquaintances, and strangers called the workforce. They are the talent you, me and other entrepreneurs will eventually need in order to ensure that our businesses survive and thrive. The catch-22 is that their behavior can build up the company's reputation or tear it down.

Luckily, there are clever ways to deal with this conundrum. Very early in the game, you have to learn how to identify business talent the way Gordy could identify future stars. Sometimes, making the right selection will be obvious. You conduct a probing interview, double-check references, notice the way the prospective employee is dressed. But your personal impressions, though important, are not foolproof. Over the years, I have developed my own talent acquisition philosophy based on five solid rules:

1. **The Jockey's Your Best Bet:** When it comes to identifying talent that I want to partner with or invest in, I don't bet on the horse. I bet on the jockey. The jockey is the one who makes a business endeavor work. I want to know: How hungry is the jockey? How bad does the jockey want

it? Is the jockey prepared to grind 24/7 and put all of his or her worldly possessions into the deal? To me, the jockey is the most challenging component of business success. Temperament and resilience are critical parts of a jockey's character composite as well, because I've found that most people can't handle failure, nor can they handle success. That's why the vast majority of people who win state lotteries in the U.S. are broke within a few years.

2. **Check Out the IQ and the EQ:** I hire for brains, and then I try to motivate. I also consciously look for people who are smarter than I am. In defining "smart," academic degrees are helpful – but not always. Things like common sense and emotional quotient (EQ) are also important parts of an individual's intellectual makeup. Regarding that hunger I spoke of earlier, I've observed over the years that jockeys who are second, third, and fourth generation college graduates are often not as hungry as individuals who are the first in their families to graduate from college.

3. **Know a Person's "Flavor Straw":** I study people and figure out what makes them tick. I observe what makes them laugh and what makes them mad. I notice the way they dress and the kinds of things they talk about. This helps me to understand them and influence them. For instance, people who know me are aware that I'll happily get up and go out to the library, but it might take some coaxing to get me to the gym. Reading is the flavor I enjoy inhaling through my straw. Noted psychologist, Abraham Maslow, best known for his Hierarchy of Needs theory, said you motivate people by determining what keeps them going

beyond six months or 12 months. Inspire your employees by learning their "flavor straw." Is it money, recognition, or being with the *in* crowd? Whatever it is, assist them in their quest to find it. If someone likes Diet Pepsi, you wouldn't bring that person ginger ale. In my case, send me knowledge through articles and books. Warning: When you analyze people, use the information you have gleaned to influence them positively. Never use it as a tool for manipulation.

4. **Give and Take:** Anyone who has children knows that some children behave better when you promise them a reward, such as a new toy or an outing. But others couldn't care less. You can promise them the moon and their grades and their attitude won't budge. In a case like that, you try taking something away. Telling them they can't play their favorite video game or watch a movie will have more impact than a gift. The same thing applies to the workforce. Some employees are out for the bonuses, the convenient parking space, being named *Office Worker of the Month*. Others will work harder just to avoid penalties and hold on to their job.

5. **Encouragement:** There are many languages in the world, but one that is universal is a plain old-fashioned smile. A smile can transform someone's day—including your own. We all have different methods of encouraging one another, but I've been told that my approach is unique. I like walking up to young people and stating point blank, "I have a deal for you. I'll give you $10 if you can answer a question." Then I bombard them with various questions

about history or everyday life until I find one they can answer. Money is not the important thing here. This is just my way of saying, "Hey, bro, it's going to be alright. You have to stay in the game!"

Of course, this is my own homespun philosophy. I didn't find it in a book, but I did come up with it after a few good and not-so-good experiences forced me to reflect on the example set by my numbers-running Uncle Paul. Yes, I'm talking about him again. He was a character, this is true. But his old-school wit is the slide rule I use when I need to boost employee morale.

Uncle Paul never attended business school, but he had a good feel for what worked and what didn't. One of his chief skills was how to interact with people and how to make them feel like a valuable part of the process. Oh, and he never forgot about that "flavor straw." When he made his rounds to pick up the numbers, his conversations usually went something like this:

"Good morning, Miss Wilson. How are you doing, Miss Wilson? Did you see what happened yesterday on 'Search for Tomorrow?' Can you believe that? By the way, that will be $2.20. Miss Wilson, how's your granddaughter? She doing alright? Ok, see you tomorrow."

Don't think for a minute that Uncle Paul liked soap operas. Of course he didn't. But Uncle Paul knew how to relate to people. He knew he could connect with them by dangling their favorite carrot. As a result, his customers, and the people he hired, tended to have his back. Meanwhile, they were certain that he had theirs. It doesn't get any easier than that. Today, in the global market of conglomerates and multifaceted corporations, the same approach is being utilized, just in different ways. Uncle Paul's habit of catering to the interests of his base is no different than a sales manager lavishing praise on the highest grossing members of his sales team. It just makes good business sense to treat people well if you expect them to do a good job.

Now let's take this a step further. Treating people well extends beyond perks like company cars and trips to the Bahamas. It's as plain and simple as the floor beneath your feet. I mean that literally. Just look around at various office spaces and you'll see that contemporary entrepreneurs are going out of their way to include creature comforts that make the job site so appealing, some workers don't want to go home. I'm not suggesting you install colorful, winding playground slides and some of the other trappings you hear about in Silicon Valley. But I am saying it's not a bad idea to create an atmosphere that your employees find enticing.

A firm's specific work environment must represent its corporate culture, but that doesn't mean the environment has to be boring. Take Vitec Automotive, my favorite among the many companies I have launched. Vitec, which I had the pleasure of selling in 2015, actually had a gym on the premises. My partners and I had it installed because the plant operated 24 hours a day, seven days a week. Another hallmark of Vitec was that our employee cubicles had an open-air, bullpen-style layout—similar to that found at Bloomberg L.P., which Michael Bloomberg also employed in New York's City Hall during the time he was mayor.

Vitec's C-suite offices were located all the way at the end of the office floor. This meant I had to walk through the cubicles to get to my office, which gave me an opportunity to fraternize with my employees about both personal and business matters. It removed bureaucratic layers and barriers and enabled me and my employees to form deeper connections. I'm a people person, so this allowed me to exercise one of my strengths. In some ways I might have been more thrilled about the layout than my employees. After all, it was a far cry from the way I started out. For decades, there were no office spaces at McDonald's and I had to store the company check ledgers in the trunk of my car. That was my office. When McDonald's finally began to create real offices inside the franchises, it placed them in the basement. Who gets excited about going to a basement office?

With this in mind, I set out to blend the corporate culture of my flagship enterprise, Vitec, into the work space. A great deal of planning and thought went into everything, from every office's physical layout to how talent was acquired and developed. But at the automotive assembly plant we operate in Alabama, my partners and I had to consider different factors, such as practical logistics. There are no gas stations, diners, or convenience stores with cigarettes and alcohol for miles outside of the plant. This was deliberately planned to encourage focus and maximum productivity among employees. It prevents employees from taking long lunch breaks, sometimes drinking cans of beer, then returning to the plant impaired and suboptimal.

There's a big difference between an aesthetically-pleasing work environment and an environment filled with distractions that are not conducive to productivity. If you recall my earlier reference to Monday morning cars, you'll understand this decision and others. It could be a thumbs-up on ping pong tables, which have become clichéd shorthand for the more relaxed nature of tech startup life. Or it could be like our plant in Alabama, a highly-controlled environment where everything the employees need during the workday is found onsite. Companies must create the kind of office and campus setting that aligns with their corporate values.

Back in the '80s when Jheri curls and large, door knocker earrings were popular, my McDonald's franchise partners and I had a strict policy forbidding those styles. Our employees were told up front that the styles were against the rules and not part of the image we wanted to project. Whenever an employee would pipe up and say, "that's illegal," I'd reply, "you let me worry about that."

You have to set the tone at the top, and that's exactly what we did. Every morning we held leadership meetings that were productive, professional, and tightly run. As leaders, we knew we had to understand our own strengths and weaknesses and build in habits and practices that aligned with our natural rhythms. We also knew that we had to understand the strengths and weaknesses of our employees in order to encourage them to use their full potential.

It wasn't easy but, as Nelson Mandela once said, "It always seems impossible until it is done." I always knew it could be done because I'm a firm believer that you have to give more in order to get the maximum. So, I invest in my staff as well as my businesses. I used to reward my most trusted long-term managers by assigning them the task of getting my next company up and running—and giving them a combination of a salary and a 5 percent equity stake consisting of phantom stock as compensation. Unlike traditional stock, those who have phantom stock are not eligible to vote at shareholder meetings.

Once the new company was up and running and had achieved some milestones and profitability, I would give that manager real stock, where he or she was allowed to vote. As the company grew, I would reward him or her with additional real stock.

When I was ready to launch my next company, we would start the process all over again. I'm known for being generous, some would say to a fault. When I sold Vitec, I gave my employees more money than was required. But it never troubled me because I am blessed and I wanted to bless my employees as well. On the flipside, every CEO has experienced employee malfeasance and I'm no exception.

Two major incidents come to mind. At Vitec, the business I loved the most, I experienced corporate fraud by an extremely intelligent young man who had passed the CPA exam at age 21. He was a member of the same fraternal order that I belonged to and was recommended by an employee I trusted. That trust and high-level recommendation gave him entrée to a major role within Vitec. If it were not for the referral, possibly, I would have followed my gut.

Something told me not to hire him because he was too flashy for my taste, and flashy is an odd trait for a finance guy. When my worst fears came to pass—the guy stole from us—I didn't beat up on myself. I simply reminded myself that Michael Jordan used to practice free throws while blindfolded. He was honing his skills, perfecting his judgment, tuning in to the precise maneuver. That's something all of us have to do. It's a nonstop learning process.

Years ago, a CEO who was my star employee left one of my companies and my partners and I had to avert another near disaster. The initial mould that creates an automotive part we produce is expensive to build. We discovered that the new CEO we hired was having low-quality moulds produced by one of his friends in Wisconsin, and pocketing the difference. This unethical CEO died unexpectedly. We had a $100,000 company life insurance policy on him, but his family had no personal insurance policy and his wife ended up in great financial distress. We also found out that his son was involved in the theft.

When his widow phoned me about her situation, I met with her, listened to what she had to say, and replied, "Mrs. X, you knew who your husband was better than I did—and that he had a proclivity to do certain things. I will get back to you." I gave her half of the $100,000 policy. News that I had chosen to take the honorable route to help the widow of a man who was less than honorable to our company rapidly spread throughout the supplier community. I didn't concern myself with who he was because I know who I am—and that I would continue to be blessed and get that money back in multiples.

My master's degree is in social work and I remain a social worker at heart. I know that when it comes to an individual's character, ethics and integrity are the bedrock. This has always been an integral part of my hiring philosophy and the basis for the way I relate to employees, including managers. What this means is that I am deft in analyzing people and I cue in on what makes sense, and those things in someone's profile that are at odds or amiss. I also stay on the lookout for what's known as "good fits" and "bad fits." I've seen bad fits undermine the careers of some very talented individuals.

Once, I hired a CFO who had earned an undergraduate degree from the University of Maryland and a master of business administration from Harvard University—the perfect background for our company. Or so I thought. This guy showed up at work one day wearing a black shoe on one foot and a brown shoe on the other. His odd habits didn't end with his personal appearance. When you were unfortunate to ride in his car, you felt like you were sitting in the junk-hauling truck from the 70's sitcom, *Sanford and Son*. He had a first-rate mind, but his lack of social skills held him back from working in places like Wall Street. Eventually, he wound up in China working for a major national company. I shudder at the fact that there are so many who lose out on opportunities and promotions because they cannot make the cultural and social leap needed to be a "good" fit.

A "good fit" means the individual is a team player who has the appropriate mindset and a clear understanding of the corporate culture. These are essential traits for employees. When it comes to a business partner, these traits are so important, they're not even negotiable. If you decide to partner with someone, make sure the two of you have shared values that can translate into a harmonious working relationship. Ask yourself:

- Do they have good rapport with you and the rest of the management team?

- Can they handle stress?

- Are they insubordinate?

- Can they go with the flow?

- Are they trustworthy?

- Do they have a history of loyalty?

Keep in mind that a business partnership is like a marriage. It can bring out the best in you or the worst in you. Compatible partners push one another's talents to the surface by playing off one another's strengths. Magic Johnson was a better basketball player when he played against Larry Bird, and Bird was better when he played against Magic. When a sharp knife meets a sharp knife both knives become sharper—or, as the Bible puts it, "iron sharpens iron."

Some individuals are born salespeople, but a born salesperson without some training and feedback from management and colleagues can be a loose cannon. Likewise, some people are just natural talent-finders and, by employing their interpersonal skills, are able to seek out the best in people. They, too, need formal training and feedback to refine their skills.

In an ideal business relationship, the company flourishes. In a bad one, tempers flare, money is lost and businesses are liquidated. The goal of a good partnership is mutual respect and understanding. And to achieve that, you will have to operate within certain parameters that everyone has agreed are in the best interests of the company.

If that's not the case, do not enter into a partnership. Period. Clearly, they are not for everyone. Before jumping into one, you should ask yourself if you really need it, and why. I have found that there are three legitimate reasons for a partnership:

- You need more money.

- You have the money, but you need a complementary partner who fills in the talent gap.

- Political expediency.

If you don't fall into any of these categories, a partnership might not be for you. But if you determine that a partnership is your cup of tea, make sure you actually know this person and know him or her well. Make sure this person is someone who can efficiently execute plans and handle being in the midst of a storm. Make sure you are going by what you have experienced (as in working with this person in the past) and not what you have heard. After you have dotted your "i's" and crossed all of your "t's," you'll be ready to offer Joe Blow an equity stake in your firm.

Sylvester Hester, my business partner of nearly 30 years, has started several companies for me, employing the method I mentioned earlier. I would give him 5 percent phantom stock. The business would grow. He would hit some home runs. I would then give him "real," or voting, stock. He would hit some more home runs. I would give him more real stock, then he would move on to our next startup business and do the same.

Sylvester is trustworthy and, as a result, we have a great relationship. He joined Regal Plastics in 1987 after being the first Black student to graduate from Ferris State University with a degree in plastics engineering. We soon discovered that he had a natural ability to sell. This filled a major talent gap. Between 1991 and 1996, Regal went from a company with $13 million in sales to $33 million in sales. As Sylvester likes to tell it, this occurred at a time when globalization was affecting the interaction between automotive companies and suppliers. Under this new model, automotive suppliers were not paid until the end of the year. Everything was about cost containment. Tier one suppliers became tier two suppliers to larger companies.

As this new trend progressed, tier one companies began

to outsource their non-core businesses and most aspects of the core business they brought in-house. Meanwhile, the auto business was moving to the South. In 1998, Sylvester relocated to Atlanta, Georgia and started ARD Logistics. Johnson Controls was the first tier one company to outsource its logistics to us. This was a major home run. In 2001, Sylvester hit another home run with a contract for our plant in Alabama and, again, in 2003 with the opening of the ARD office in Charleston, South Carolina.

With each success, he received a larger share of the companies he started. ARD Logistics continues to diversify into food and beverage, aerospace, and the government sector. Over the past 30 years, Sylvester has worked to earn his new title of President and CEO of Global Alliance, the umbrella company for most of my automotive companies.

However, I'm at a point in my life—and our partnership—where I'm not open to taking on more risk. In order to expand your business, a bank will want you to back a loan with a personal guarantee. This means if the loan goes under, you will be expected to write the check to cover it. To minimize the potential of such a problem, I created a special arrangement with Sylvester and the bank. Under this arrangement, he is taking the business in a direction of growth and he and I are handling the necessary guarantees in a more equitable manner. As a result, Sylvester will become the primary manager and owner at a future date.

If I'm a majority owner in a business, I try to be hands-on. I have to be personally involved and vested. I'm not going to be in Florida and have my partner managing a company with my million dollars on the line, even though we've known each other so long he can practically count my money. Trust is not the issue here; it is my lack of appetite for extra risks. As has happened with me and my business partner, who is decades younger than I am, there's a point when the difference in age and number of years each partner has been in business can come into play. I don't need additional growth to maintain my current lifestyle. Revenue from my current portfolio of companies amply covers all my business and personal needs.

Any partnerships I still maintain are a matter of choice. Just as I knew how to get into them, I also know how to get out. This is a basic business skill: You have to know when to hold them and when to fold them. Part of creating a business is also developing an exit strategy, where you and any partners agree on one or more desired future outcomes for the business, such as a merger, an initial public offering (IPO) or a sale. One of the ways to benefit from a business is to build it and sell it. The latter is known as harvesting. In a partnership, this can become problematic. What do you do if you want to harvest the business in your exit strategy and your partner isn't ready to harvest? This is common, especially among partners in different age or life cycles. To avoid clashing, a company must take two critical steps in advance.

STEP ONE: HAVE A BUY/SELL AGREEMENT IN PLACE

This agreement should establish that, one day, one of the partners is going to exit the business. The company should be prepared for this financially and operationally.

STEP TWO: BE PREPARED FOR A PARTNER'S UNTIMELY DEATH

The family of a deceased partner may know that, prior to death, he or she had a $3 million equity stake in the company. That might be true, but that doesn't necessarily mean that the company has $3 million in liquid assets to compensate the spouse of the deceased for that ownership stake. Companies typically fund them via insurance policies. This measure should be addressed in the buy/sell agreement.

Without these agreements, handling or dissolving a partnership can be as challenging as the rockiest marriage or the most bitter divorce. Yet I must admit, in a good union, the benefits far outweigh the problems. Partnerships allow those involved to divide and multiply. One partner is charged primarily with internal matters related to the company's business (Mr. or Mrs. Inside), while the other focuses on external matters (Mr. or Mrs. Outside). One of you is taking care of operations and personnel while the other is focused on finance and sales. One is hunting and the other is skinning. The roles are distinct but complementary.

You even see this in the typical university environment which has a provost who deals with the professors, and a president who goes out and raises money. It's an inside-outside division of labor. One person has his hands in and the other has his hands out. Why is that so important? I can answer that with a story that would raise the eyebrows of any savvy entrepreneur.

One of my young mentees wanted to open up a Burger King or a McDonald's franchise with his two brothers. Their father had died a few years earlier and, collectively, they had $400,000 in seed capital. They lived in Flint, Michigan, but made frequent visits to Lansing, Michigan. From my mentee's perspective, Lansing was an excellent franchise site because he and his brothers had enough revenue to hire someone to relocate to the city and operate the restaurant for them.

I took a deep breath, then asked, "Where's your wife?"

He replied, "She's here in the house."

I said, "Put her on the phone. I want to talk to her."

He wasn't sure what to say. After a brief pause, he responded, "Why you want to speak with my wife?"

I replied, "I want to tell her she married a d--- fool! Think about what you just told me. You're going to take $400,000 of your family's money and hire somebody to go to Lansing and operate your business while you go to work every day. What makes you think that's going to work?"

"People do it every day," he answered.

"Trust me," I said. "I've been in this business almost 50 years. If I ran your restaurant, and I ran it very well, I would suck up the little bit of profit you make—and you wouldn't notice it. I would "fee" you to death. I would have management fees and I would have my cousin on the payroll."

He didn't get it, but one of his brothers did. That sibling called back and said, "My brother told me what you said to him. Thank you very much."

Be very clear if you're starting a business: *You have to manage your own business.*

That's the mentality of so many people: *I'm going to have somebody else manage my business.*

In my line of work, I'm frugal and practical. I'm not going to invest in anything I'm not a part of operationally. There may come a time when you can hire and begin to outsource some of the tasks, but by that time you will know every pore, fiber, and tick of your business. Outsourcing only makes sense if you're making enough to absorb the management fees and still turn a healthy profit.

I could have taken a more step-by-step approach by talking to my mentee about the dangers of absentee management, but I went for the jugular and basically told him: "You're crazy! I own five McDonald's and five other businesses around the country, and I can guarantee you that, at this very moment, there is someone in one of my businesses acting like an owner and taking profits, or materials, or French fries, or drinks that they do not own. And they're giving it away." That's what corporate jargon refers to as shrinkage.

One of my young employees casually told me a story about how she had run out of money and her girlfriend who worked at a sandwich shop gave her something to eat for free. This was an example of an employee generously gifting something that he or she does not own. Another young McDonald's employee at my Grosse Pointe, Michigan, location gave away a free soda to a visiting friend while I was there. When I pointed out what she had done she said, "Dr. Pickard. That's my friend. I just gave him a Coke." Because that was her friend, she felt it was not stealing. I kindly, but firmly, let her know that it was.

This brings me back to my original point. Your business is in the hands of your Finders, Minders, and Grinders. Choose them wisely, treat them with respect, but only give them as much rope as they need. You are the eyes, ears, and brains behind your establishment. You're the person steering the ship and shepherding the crew. That might mean a whole lot of hours and more sacrifices than you anticipated. But there are only three ways for those with talent and ambition to get to their destination: Crawl, Walk, and then Run.

PRINCIPLE SIX: FAILURE

"In every adversity lies the seed of an equal or greater opportunity."
—Napoleon Hill

I waited. It was the year 2000 and I was a participant in a one-day entrepreneur conference at Harvard University in Boston. But I had a special concern and no one had addressed it. So I kept waiting. Hundreds of people streamed in and out of the assembly rooms. Meanwhile, speaker after speaker discussed project management, joint ventures, employee retention, spreadsheets.

I continued to wait.

The next talk I attended dealt with global enterprise. As a business owner with global reach, I found it highly beneficial. But it wasn't the food my soul craved.

I waited.

Another hour passed, the convention ended and I returned home, puzzled. Every presenter had talked about success, but not a single one had touched on that hidden little fear that lurks in the back of all entrepreneurs' minds: What happens if I fail?

What should I do when the doors slam, when the bottom falls out, when all loan applications have been denied?

I wasn't exactly a neophyte in this area. Although my Mc-Donald's franchises were thriving and my auto supply businesses were doing well, I had recently come frighteningly close to financial paralysis. I pulled through without a scar. But, I'm a realist. I wanted to be equipped in case there was a repeat experience. And don't forget, I had been schooled by the best of them, my Uncle Paul. He was a pragmatist who warned me that businesses are always a risk. According to my wise old uncle, anyone who stays in the game long enough will stare rejection, disappointment and, possibly bankruptcy, in the face.

That's why I was disappointed in the agenda at that conference. I had hoped to receive a few tips about remaining positive while on the brink of defeat. I was interested in hearing someone explain the cyclical nature of entrepreneurship and tell me how to weather the winds of change if, once again, they should happen to blow my way. What I hadn't anticipated was avoidance and denial. I didn't realize the topic would be swept under the rug.

Fortunately, attitudes have flip-flopped since then. Today, failure is being examined, even romanticized. In order to prepare students for the "real" world, failure is an elective course at certain universities and high schools. In fact, the School of the Art Institute of Chicago, encourages students to enroll in the class, "The Ethics and Aesthetics of Failure."

It doesn't stop there. Failure is the subject of newspaper and magazine articles and a popular theme in contemporary motivational lectures. So much ado is being made about it, you might find yourself wondering if it has become *en vogue*. It has not. But what has occurred is an acceptance of the vicissitudes of life, business endeavors included.

These days there is a tacit realization that failure is something that simply comes with the entrepreneurship territory. It's like gravity. Sometimes you fall and, well, falling is natural. All you have to do is get up. When you do, you'll be comforted by the awareness that your situation wasn't so bad after all. In fact, you just joined a pretty impressive club.

Did you know that Oprah Winfrey was fired from one of her first TV news reporter jobs because she wasn't the "right fit"? Or that billionaire author J.K. Rowling was a welfare recipient and her blockbuster *Harry Potter* novel was rejected by 12 publishers? Then there's our nation's 16th president, Abraham Lincoln. Before he made it to the White House, he lost seven elections and struck out in business three times.

Yet, they were not deterred. Their names are well known today because they understood one of life's most valuable lessons: If at first you don't succeed, you're about average.

Winfrey, Rowling, and Lincoln knew that failure is not the exception, it is the rule. They didn't allow their careers to be destroyed or their drive to be dampened by that dreaded little life episode that eventually knocks on everyone's door. They realized that failure is as American as apple pie and Chevrolet. It is not a death sentence. It is not the enemy, and it is not the last word. According to the Small Business Administration, around 33 percent of all new ventures close down within two years and about 50 percent are out of business in five years. Only one in four is still around 15 years after opening. Yet, many are successful when they stay the course and dare to cast their net again and again. As novelist F. Scott Fitzgerald once said, "Never confuse a single defeat with a final defeat." Jazz legend Miles Davis said something similar. In his own enigmatic way, Miles remarked: "When you hit a wrong note, it's the next note you play that determines if it's good or bad."

As an entrepreneur, that "next note" is up to you. You can let your mistakes engulf you or you can keep pressing forward. In his effort to create a light bulb, Thomas Edison failed nearly 1,000 times. But Edison, who had been told by his teachers that he was "too stupid to learn anything," had developed pretty thick skin by then. He saw all of his efforts as a success. He said he had merely discovered 1,000 ways not to achieve his goal.

Think about the top 10 entrepreneurs in the United States. Virtually all of them failed once or twice in a business venture due to lack of knowledge or funding. In some cases, a misstep placed them so far behind the market's conditions that they were forced to leave the race. Temporarily. There's a big difference between leaving and quitting. Make no mistake about it: success is the kissing cousin of failure. The people on top are there because they refused to remain on the bottom. These rags-to-riches, failure-before-success stories include:

- **Tyler Perry.** From 1992 to 1998, every stage play Perry produced failed. In most cases, he lost all of the money he had invested and in some instances, not a single person showed up for the performance. Tyler said that each time a production did poorly he "learned something new." He would apply what he learned to the next show and the next. In 1998, he decided to take a revamped version of his failed play, *I Know I've Been Changed*, on the road. That's when he finally found success. Eventually, Perry went from living in his car to living in a mansion and writing and producing 17 films and six television shows that have a lifetime gross of more than $845 million. He says: "What you may perceive as failure may very well be an opportunity to learn, grow, get better, and prepare for the next level."

- **Walt Disney.** A high school dropout, Disney was fired from a Missouri newspaper because his editor said he "lacked imagination." Later, he launched a business, Laugh-o-Gram Studios, which went bankrupt. One night, while broke, tired, and still pursuing his dream of animation, he noticed a mouse sitting in the middle of the shabby room he was renting. The mouse stared at Disney and, in a state of frustration, Disney stared back. He imagined the critter was saying, "Man, you're so poor you don't even have any cheese in this place." Disney doodled the mouse and it became the prototype for one of the biggest icons the cartoon industry has ever known.

- **Sidney Poitier.** At the age of 16 Bahamas native, Sidney Poitier, worked as a delivery boy in a white Miami neighborhood. Unaware of American racial politics, he made a package drop-off to the front door instead of the back door. When he returned home that evening, he was told that the Ku Klux Klan was looking for him. Poitier used his meager earnings to buy a one-way bus ticket as far from Florida as he could get. He ended up in New York. After two years of struggle, he spotted an ad for the American Negro Theater and—out of desperation—decided to try out. He failed miserably. His Caribbean accent and poor reading skills made him a laughing stock during the audition. Disgraced, Poitier found a night job as a dishwasher and spent his free time perfecting his voice inflections and honing his reading and acting skills. By the time he was 25, Poitier was starring in major motion pictures and on his way to becoming the first Black male to receive an Academy Award for Best Actor.

- **Reginald Lewis.** When he was a student at Virginia State College, Lewis had a big decision to make. Should he own up to a shoulder injury and risk losing his football scholarship and possible National Football League career? Or should he endure the pain and avoid the specter of failure? He accepted failure. Several years later, he was graduating from Harvard Law School and preparing himself for corporate America. But his first attempt to buy a business failed. Two years later, he bid on a company that manufactured lawn chairs. The bid failed. He failed again in a 1983 effort to purchase a radio station group. Lewis armed himself with knowledge by studying the details of public deals, both successful and unsuccessful. In 1984, Lewis, author of *Why Should White Guys Have All The Fun?*, bought McCall's Patterns, a sewing pattern company. After doubling its earnings, he sold it for more than twice its purchase price. Then, he won a bidding war for Beatrice International, a food conglomerate with two billion in annual sales, making him the top Black-owned business owner in the nation.

- **Tom Monaghan.** The founder and CEO of Domino's Pizza was once an example of failure personified. Monaghan grew up in a Catholic orphanage and spent much of his childhood daydreaming about owning a chain of ice cream stands or a fleet of tractors. But his early adult years were fraught with disappointment, and the business world wasn't as welcoming as he had hoped. In one instance, a potential business partner stole close to $2,000, Monaghan's life savings, and left town. Later, Monaghan started a pizza company in Ypsilanti, Michigan, with his brother. However, the two were forced to file for bankruptcy and, at one point, the struggling operation burned down. Monaghan's brother eventually gave up on the business and asked Tom to buy him out. All Tom had to offer was the little Volkswagen Beetle he used for pizza delivery. The brother accepted and Tom moved to Ann Arbor and went solo. It was there, several failures later, that his vision became reality. Today, Domino's Pizza is the second largest pizza franchise in the world. If you visit the Ann Arbor headquarters, you'll see a shiny, refurbished 1954 Volkswagen in the lobby—a monument to the power of sheer persistence.

Do you see the pattern? Real entrepreneurs don't shrink at the first sign of trouble. Real entrepreneurs buckle up and shift to a higher gear. As an up-and-comer, you must embrace both risk and opportunity, then do your personal due diligence. Decide, in advance, how you would handle it if your venture was sidetracked. Would you be humiliated or would you be ready to tackle it and bounce back? Reactions are varied because failure has a different impact depending on your background, your expectations, the number of people bragging about you, rooting for you, or eagerly anticipating your golden victory.

I still remember the time one of the instructors at the community college I once attended announced in class that a certain student had flunked out of school. I really felt for this young lady because, obviously, if you fail community college, that's pretty rock bottom. I also couldn't help but notice the look of profound sadness on our instructor's face. She explained that the student had to go home and give her parents, her siblings, her church associates, and her friends the news that she had failed.

At the time, I sort of figured the emotional aspect of failure wouldn't be that significant for me. I didn't have to factor in other people's expectations because that really wasn't on my radar screen. No one expected me to succeed. When I shattered those notions and soared to greater heights, it was a pleasant surprise for everyone, including me. This newfound success placed me on a higher pedestal and a totally different trajectory. My world changed and so did my standards, my circle, my peers. People believed in me. Newspapers were writing articles about me. I was raking in awards and flying around the country, hobnobbing with the big wheels. Things that hadn't mattered to me mattered all of a sudden.

With this adjusted perception came the pressure of wanting to make sure I didn't let anyone down. After I had at least eight or nine McDonald's franchises under my belt, I began to explore the horizon for other opportunities. A big one came in the form of Regal Plastics, a bankrupt auto supply business. Why would I buy a company that was in bankruptcy? Well, for one thing, it was cheap. For another, I firmly believed in my abilities. I assumed that the company's problems were the result of poor management.

In order to get the ball rolling, I had to meet with a committee of Regal Plastic's creditors and assure them that I had what it took to turn their lemon into lemonade. At the time, Regal Plastics was one of the few companies that produced shifter knobs for the gear sticks in automatic and stick shift cars for one of the Big Three automakers, and it was critically important to them that the fragile auto supply company survive. During my meeting, I explained how I would breathe new life into this endeavor. I also made a request to the auto supplier that the money they were owed by Regal Plastic be turned into long term debt. As part of this request, I agreed to pay back 40 cents on every dollar.

The credit committee voted unanimously to let me give it a whirl. I was ecstatic. Keep in mind, my McDonald's franchises were doing well. But I was eager to expand. Regal Plastics was my first step outside of the fast food industry and into a bold new arena.

Within a few years, my team and I had revived the business and were prepared to pay back the creditors eight months before the scheduled payoff date. My advisory committee members were so impressed they tried to convince me that, because I had turned things around in record time, the creditors would accept 10 cents on the dollar as a payback. Something about that didn't feel quite right to me. Against their wishes, I stuck with my original commitment and paid back the loan at 40 cents on the dollar. Now, the company was rocking and rolling, and my income had increased exponentially.

Little did I know, disaster was lurking in the shadows. Ten years down the road, the auto company that did business with Regal Plastics gave us a major order for the interior of a new car they were just beginning to manufacture. To fill this order, we had to go from two plants to six plants. That meant buying more buildings, hiring additional employees, and acquiring new equipment.

I saw it as an exciting prospect and a chance for tremendous progress. But my calculations and my confidence were out of sync. Regal Plastics was not ready financially or organizationally for such a huge leap. We didn't have the right people in the right places and, with our new plants and new equipment, we had taken on far too much debt. To make matters worse, the new cars didn't sell. The whole thing was a mess.

In hindsight, we should have said no to the expansion. But nobody says no when they think they're good. We were good, but, apparently, not quite that good. In plain and simple business lexicon, we were "hugging ourselves to death."

This experience, which lasted eight, long nightmarish months, turned out to be the worst of my career. My best right-hand man had already moved on to another opportunity. The car had failed. We had more debt than we could handle and we couldn't pay our creditors. Operationally, we were failing drastically.

I could say, at this point, that I sucked it up and shrugged, "hey, sh—t happens." Or that I reflected on the infamous words of author Napoleon Hill: "Every adversity, every failure, every heartache, carries with it the seed of an equal or greater benefit." I could even say that I turned to one of Michael Jordan's best known quotes: "I've missed more than 9,000 shots in my career. I've lost almost 300 games. Twenty-six times, I've been trusted to take the game winning shot and missed. I've failed over and over again in my life. And that is why I succeed."

Yes, I could say that I clung to these pearls of wisdom, but I'd be lying. For the first time on my entrepreneurial path, failure was looming before me like a dark tornado, and it depressed me in ways that I can barely explain. When you're grappling with a business fiasco, it's as harrowing as a personal crisis, but in many ways it can be worse. The public nature of your problem— the litigation, court orders, pressure from suppliers, employees, accountants, lawyers, your banker—can make it heavier. And it can cause you to withdraw. I was losing weight as well as sleep. I had no desire to go to social functions because I thought everyone knew about my ordeal.

To her credit, my fiancée did her best to encourage me. She told me that every company had problems and that I shouldn't let my business woes stop me from getting out and having fun. Still, I refused. All of my attention was riveted on an upcoming meeting that had been arranged between me and the credit committee.

I'll never forget that day. I had to drive to a hotel at Detroit Metropolitan Airport to stand in front of a group of irate creditors and try to explain what went wrong. I was so nervous, my palms were sweating and my heart was racing. I had never failed before and here I was at this very public event, hanging on by my nails.

As I approached the podium and looked into those angry eyes, I recognized many of the same individuals I had stood before 10 years earlier to make my initial pitch. Most were there— the people who supplied the cardboard boxes, the sales reps, the vendors who provided tools. Only one original creditor was missing—his position was now being handled by his son. All in all, there were about 100 men, pointing, hollering and cursing.

I cleared my throat and spoke:

"You're looking at the guy who made the decision to take

on all of this business," I said. "And it was more than we could chew."

The shouting escalated. But before I could utter another word, a guy stood up and asked everyone to calm down. (Unbeknownst to the creditors, this person was a plant who had been hired by my team to come to my defense.) The person reminded the group that I had run a successful business for 10 years and had paid them all back 40 cents on the dollar in a timely manner.

"Everyone in this room got their check and no one sent the check back," he said. "So we have made money with him. He has grown the business, tripled it in size, and he admitted he over-expanded."

He continued: "Once you finish screaming and yelling, you need to think about something. If you force him into bankruptcy, we get pennies. He's paid the money back before. That's critical. He'll pay it back again."

After another couple of weeks and a second meeting, I was granted additional time to work out Regal Plastic's problems. Within six months, I was able to orchestrate an orderly wind-down of the company so that I could eventually exit it completely. In the meantime, I began to recall my late Uncle Paul's guidance and reminded myself that failing is an intrinsic aspect of success and as much a part of being in business as securing a loan or writing a check. Often it's a step in the right direction. I also learned that failure is not the challenge. The challenge is what you do with the failure. In *"Think and Grow Rich,"* Napoleon Hill wrote: "Before success comes in any man's life, he is sure to meet with much temporary defeat and, perhaps, some failure. When defeat overtakes a man, the easiest and most logical thing to do is to quit. That is exactly what the majority of men do. More than 500 of the most successful men this country has ever known told the author their greatest success came just one step beyond the point at which defeat had overtaken them."

These are words I now live by. Obviously I've grown as a result of my experience. I'm older and I've mastered the fine art of flying like an eagle through calamities that I used to find so intimidating. I now define failure as one of the many lanes along the journey to victory. Ironically, I'm embracing a philosophy that a number of young people seem to understand very early in life.

Because of changing social trends and, of course, the internet's infinite pool of information, an increasingly healthy outlook about failure is taking root. I've met young people who are so naturally resilient, they don't seem to sweat it when the businesses they have dreamt about for years collapses on the first try. I applaud them. They have my utmost respect. And now, after nearly 50 years of entrepreneurial mountains and valleys, I, too, have a come-what-may point of view. I also have assorted gems that I have collected along the way.

I call them *The Twelve Tenets of a Good Failure*:

1. Don't be afraid of failure. As J.K. Rowling says: "It's impossible to live without failing at something unless you live so cautiously you might as well not have lived at all—in which case, you fail by default."

2. "If you're going through hell, keep going," Winston Churchill once admonished. He added, "Never give in. Never give up. Never, never, never, never!"

3. Do not wallow. Don't think "woe is me" or convince yourself that you're the only one in the world that has had this happen. There's a lot of company in this club.

4. Apply what you learned from the experience. In Henry Ford's words: "Failure is simply the opportunity to begin again, this time more intelligently."

5. Learn something from every adversity. Every mistake comes with a lesson.

6. Look for the blessing in your failure. What miracle or new opportunity does it contain? When Regal Plastics was failing, I became more concerned about my health. Someone put me in touch with Dr. Terry Gordon, and he's been my doctor, advisor, and friend ever since. I'm also far more conscious of diet and exercise than I was in the past.

7. As you leapfrog out of the chaos and onward to greater heights, visualize what victory looks like. See yourself there!

8. Maintain an attitude of gratitude. Things went wrong; so what? Don't dwell on that. Be thankful for what is going right.

9. Never lose your enthusiasm, your zest. Rev. Martin Luther King, Jr. said: "We must accept finite disappointment, but never lose infinite hope."

10. Find someone to talk to about your situation. Don't allow embarrassment to prevent you from confiding in your friends.

11. Do not wear your problems as a badge of courage, but surely don't wear them as a mournful face either. Smile and stand tall.

12. Don't start blaming Black folks, White folks, your mama or your friends. There's no honor in the blame game.

My experiences have taught me that, every day, each and every one of us is either on the verge of failure or on the verge of success. We're either going through a crisis, coming out of a crisis, or approaching a crisis we don't know about yet. When it happens, face it like a man or like a woman. You're going to have troubles. You're going to have money sometimes that you think is yours then discover that, out of the $8 million you just made, the government is going to take four million. You might find out an associate is stealing from you. You might overreach like I did and watch what you have built swiftly fall apart.

But it doesn't matter, as long as you grow. Adopt Oprah's attitude and think of it as a "moment in time."

"Go ahead, fall down," she says. "The world looks different from the ground."

In other words, chalk it up to experience, then spread your wings wide. As Maya Angelou advised, "You may encounter many defeats, but you must not be defeated. It may even be necessary to encounter some defeats to know who you are."

"Who you are" is based on the label you are using for yourself. Are you labeling yourself a winner? Or a loser? You can't steal second base if you never get off first base. So, how can you be a loser when you were heroic enough to take the dare? And, how can you be a winner if you're not in the game, the competition, the race? Think long and hard about that question. And here's another one to consider: If a person sets a brand-new world record, he or she is considered first. But what about the old record that person just beat? If the new record-setter is now first, that means the competitor who came in second place has just achieved the former world record. That sounds pretty cool to me. I don't know how anyone could possibly describe it as a lesser accomplishment.

The only failure that ever occurs is the one an individual plasters on the walls of his or her own mind. I've always been taken aback by the idea that, at one time Edwin "Buzz" Aldrin, one of the three American astronauts who made the original trip to the moon in 1969, put himself in this category. He even became an alcoholic. Neil Armstrong was the first man in the history of the world, as we know it, to actually set foot on the moon. Buzz Aldrin followed. The third astronaut, Michael Collins, hovered above the moon in a vessel dubbed the Columbia.

Yet, it's been said that Aldrin didn't take kindly to being second. He also felt sort of awkward because his step down onto the moon's rugged surface was less than graceful. He miscalculated the gravitational pull, didn't leap high enough, and missed a step by an inch. That near slip stirred up some moon dust, causing it to settle around the legs of his space suit. This was a minor embarrassment and a hint at possible imperfection. That's heavy, isn't it? He walked on the moon and yet, at one point, thought of himself as not quite measuring up.

So my questions are: What determines whether or not one has failed? On the flipside, what is the definition of success? I mean, how does it look, and who makes that decision anyway? I think the answers lie somewhere in the punch line of an old sports joke.

A couple of players on a community baseball team were arguing furiously. One claimed the pitcher had thrown a ball and the other said: "You're crazy! That was a strike." They went back-and-forth, stamping their feet and loudly making their case. Suddenly, they heard a deep, gravelly voice. It was the umpire and, man, was he irritated. He glared at both of the men and growled:

"It ain't nothing until I call it!"

I am that umpire. You are that umpire. Others may shout "loser," but that's their opinion. I make the calls in my life and I don't see "out" as an option. And neither should you. Starting a business is tough. I agree. Staying in business is a whole lot tougher. But the beat goes on. That means you'll be just fine. All you have to do is remember one simple thing:

Failure is never fatal and success is never final.

PRINCIPLE SEVEN: FAITH

"Faith is taking the first step when you don't see the whole staircase."
—Rev. Martin Luther King, Jr.

The aroma of ripe Georgia peaches was wafting through the air, and the backyard swallows were chirping so loudly they might as well have joined the church choir. I sat up straight and tried to ignore the distractions. Dressed in my Sunday best, I was sitting in the cramped auditorium of Thomastown School and feeling kind of sweaty. It was early summer and it was downright hot. But there was an amazing speaker standing on the stage and despite my discomfort, he had my undivided attention.

I was graduating from eighth grade and here was Otis Moss, a student from the esteemed Morehouse College, giving the commencement address. I was much too young to grasp everything he was saying or to understand that Morehouse was only 60 miles away. But I was mesmerized by his words.

He said that every one of us—small town kids from the red hills of Troup County—could grow up and be anything in the world. At first I didn't believe him, but then again he had to know what he was talking about. After all, he attended Morehouse and, to a kid growing up in LaGrange, Georgia, during the 1950s, meeting someone from Morehouse was like meeting an NBA player. In my neck of the woods, he was like a celebrity and, here he was, giving us a pep talk.

He told us to reach higher and higher. He said we were smart. We could achieve. He ended by saying that success would be ours and when it happened, we must serve.

"If you have success with no service," he said "you are worse than a thief and a robber."

I held on to his message. It became the kindle for the fire that would light my way and teach me the true meaning of faith. I began to realize that faith is not just the belief you hold in God, faith is how you follow that belief. It is your inspiration, the fuse that is electrified when you create new goals and expand your dreams. It's the spark that pushes you to stay the course.

Faith was already a big part of my world back then. The fact is, it was my whole world. If you grew up in the south at this time, you were in a neighborhood, a parish, or an enclave where people told you constantly that you were special and that you were going to college. Once a month, our principal, Mr. Griggs, would assemble all the little boys in a separate classroom. (The girls went elsewhere and I have no idea what was said to them.) The boys were told we were going to Morehouse. In my case, Mr. Griggs would say I was going to graduate from Morehouse and become a preacher. I believed this for years.

All that changed when I turned 14 and my family moved to Flint, Michigan, Suddenly, my confidence and fundamental beliefs were shattered. In Flint, I had to try to adjust to an integrated school and classes that were a bit more advanced than my schoolwork in rural Georgia. For the first time in my life, I was competing with both Black and White students. Most of them were ahead of me academically and socially, and I got caught up in trying to prove myself. I guess I was plagued by the idea that I wasn't cool enough. My Southern diction wasn't big-city enough. Instead of perceiving myself as smart, I saw myself as a country boy who stuttered occasionally and couldn't keep pace with his urban peers. Distracted by a new environment, I forgot all about Morehouse and the ideology that had been instilled in me for years.

It took quite a while, but eventually, I began to pull together all the fractured pieces and rebuild my broken self image. When I did, I discovered that the faith cultivated during my early years was still my core, the divine glue that held everything in my life together.

This realization turned out to be the most important aspect of my personal growth and the crux of my eventual success. When I jumped on the business scene in my late 20s, my partners and I had very little money. We worked hard, we partied "like it was 1999," and we all believed in God. That faith enabled us to knock on Wall Street's door and shoot for excellence. I feel it should be that way for every newbie. It's difficult to build a business without a formidable belief system. As an entrepreneur, you absolutely must have faith in something, faith when things are picture-perfect, and faith when it all goes haywire.

Take FedEx founder Frederick Smith, for instance. While he was still a student at Yale University, Smith had already devised his plan to revolutionize the package delivery industry. But when he wrote about it in a term paper, his professor scoffed at the idea and graded the assignment a measly "C."

Smith wasn't swayed. In the early 1970s, he launched FedEx, the first company of its kind to rely on vans, airplanes, and posting stations to rush parcels to homes and businesses across the country overnight. The company took off like a rocket then, suddenly, began to fizzle. A few months later, Smith found himself with a $24,000 fuel debt and only $5,000 in his company's bank account.

Now this is where the situation gets tricky.

Smith had something known as fervor. He had audacity. He was filled with imagination, tenacity, and a quiet little passion called hope. Put them all together and they spell F.A.I.T.H. The young entrepreneur flew to Las Vegas with his last $5,000 and gambled it all on the blackjack table. On Monday morning, he returned to his office with $27,000 in winnings—enough to pay the fuel bill and prevent his business from going bankrupt.

The lesson to be learned here is that there is nothing stronger, and more amazing, than the power of intention. When you intend to make something happen, your mind is made up and a made-up mind has often been defined as one of the most potent forces in the universe. In the jargon of contemporary positive thinking, this means that where thought goes, a whole lot of energy flows. You become magnetized to your goal because you firmly believe in it.

You are demonstrating that unswerving faith defined by the Bible as the "substance of things hoped for, the evidence of things not seen". When you're that convinced about something, it has to happen. Why? You're free of doubt. You have embraced the object of your desire and decreed it in the name of a power higher than yourself.

In my case, that higher power is God Almighty. I'm not knocking Smith. His actions, though unconventional, saved his business. But because faith in God is the backbone of my existence, I know for sure that I would not have placed my trust in Vegas. When problems are mounting, I take them to The Cross. I spend time in prayer, calling on the God I know can fix anything.

However, faith is an individual thing, expressed in countless ways. Some tap into it by means of their own willpower and self-confidence while others turn to prayer, meditation and/or religious services in a mosque, synagogue, temple, or church. Whatever your choice, you need the support of something greater than womankind and mankind—be it God, Allah, Jehovah, Yahweh, Buddha, or Divine Energy. When the cash flow is low and you're grasping at straws, sometimes the only thing you can do is seek out spiritual solace and hold on to the promise of grace.

George Shirley, the first Black tenor to sing a leading role with the Metropolitan Opera, is an exquisite example of this. Shirley, who once worked at a Detroit high school where he taught voice lessons to Motown artists Diana Ross, Smokey Robinson, and Mary Wilson, carved out a beautiful niche for himself in a profession that was not always kind to Black performers. I once had the honor of meeting Shirley and he told me something that gave me chills. He said he succeeded against the odds because he had an abiding faith that was fueled by his link to those who walked before him.

"My people were slaves," he said. "God placed within them a voice box for music and a seed and drive for music they could not fully express. And here I am more than 100 years later with the genes, the physical structure, the lungs, and the opportunity to maximize this gift."

Shirley went on to say that his belief in God was deepened each time he sang, for every time he exercised his vocal chords, he was engaging in a sacred experience—bringing alive the pain, the beauty and the faith of his African American ancestors.

As Maya Angelou so eloquently wrote in her poem, *And Still I Rise*: "I am the dream and the hope of the slave. I rise. I rise. I rise." Faith is a highly personal form of rising to the occasion. It's a lofty moniker for a trust that tugs at each spirit and summons us to different missions. But for everyone, it serves the same purpose: To instill calmness in the midst of strife. To empower. To demonstrate the impossible. To create a profound connection to God.

Believe me, when you hit those financial potholes and the rubber meets the road, you have to find something to guide you. I happen to believe God always sends an angel, an interceptor, a message, a symbol. Sometimes you're so overwhelmed you can't see it, can't feel it or hear it. That's when you have to get quiet and listen to that small voice within. As songwriter/gospel vocalist James Cleveland sings, "Peace be still." Sometimes, you just have to be still. Then you have to know in your heart that what you're requesting has already happened.

In *Mark 11:24*, the Bible states: "Therefore I say unto you, what things so ever ye desire, when ye pray, believe that ye receive them, and ye shall have them."

How can you tell whether or not you are truly living in faith? A pastor I know once explained it as a knowledge from within that no one can erase. This pastor said he had a vision that his seven-year-old son would, one day, become a professional football player. To help his son train, he videotaped football games. Of course, like any fan, he saved the games that ended in a victory for his favorite team.

In one of his sermons, the pastor—whose son made it all the way to the NFL —compared his faith to the way he experiences a televised rerun of a sporting event. Although he knows how it's going to end, he reacts to every play. When a player fumbles the ball, he yells, "Oh, No!" When a player leaps in the air and catches a long one, he shouts, "Oh, Yeah! That's what I'm talkin' about!"

He's aware of the winning team because the game was taped and the outcome had already been revealed on ESPN and the six o'clock news. But he allows himself to move through a range of emotions and get the feel of the live game. He sees this practice as an analogy for everyday life.

"During my down times, I know God is going to deliver," he explained. "But I got to go through each stage—the ups, the downs, the sideways, the push backs, the setbacks. But I know how it's going to end."

This is the same approach that's been helpful for me. My deep-seated faith tells me that God is gathering all the pieces and patching them back together. Yet, I still have to climb the hills and swim through the creeks. After Regal Plastics failed, there was no message louder and clearer than that. I had pulled through the debacle, gotten my emotions back on track and even made a deal with a company that wanted to buy one of the plants. Then, at the last minute, the buyer pulled out and left me strapped with a $900,000 debt.

But my ordeal was over and I knew it. In my heart, I was

sure everything would be A-OK. As I made phone calls, reached out to my network and followed the proper protocol, I was simply going through the motions like my pastor friend. All the while, I spoke like it was going to work out. I acted like I knew it was going to work out. I believed it was going to work out—and it did.

That's the best kind of faith—faith in action. In his book, *Love, Medicine & Miracles*, Dr. Bernie Siegel writes: "When you suffer a misfortune, you are faced with the choice of what to do with it. You can wring good from it, or more pain."

He goes on to say: "Spirituality, unconditional love and the ability to see that pain and problems are opportunities for growth and redirection—these things allow us to make the best of the time we have … We see that there is no real past or future, and that as soon as we start thinking in terms of past and future, regretting, and wishing—we lose ourselves in judgmental thinking."

Indeed, we have the power to change our lives, overcome hardships, and heal ourselves—through faith. Study after study shows heart patients recovering, cancer patients surviving, even crops growing better when they have been the target of ongoing prayer. Dr. Dale Matthews, a Maryland physician and author of *The Faith Factor*, analyzed more than 200 studies linking faith to health. He says that prayer reduces the chance of illness and speeds recovery time for those who are healing from surgery and debilitating diseases. Meanwhile, Dr. Harold Koenig, of Duke University, says prayer inhibits cortisol and other stress hormones that have a negative impact on the immune system. By the same token, he believes faith floods the immune system with peace.

We're not talking barrels of faith. According to scripture, you need less than a drop: "And the Lord said, if ye had faith as a grain of mustard seed, ye might say unto this sycamine tree, be thou plucked up by the root, and be thou planted in the sea; and it should obey you.

You only need the faith of a mustard seed." *Luke 17:6*

On one of my many visits to Atlanta, I observed this first-hand. There was a news story on TV about an armed robbery at a restaurant. A reporter was interviewing the fearless woman whose quick thinking helped save the lives of the people who worked at a steakhouse she managed. When the news station played back the tape of her 911 call, I listened carefully and couldn't get over the peace in her voice. The reporter asked how she had remained so calm and she replied that she owed it to her corporate training. Yet I knew better. She was walking by faith. I don't know what name she gave it or what shaped her beliefs, but it was clear to me that she had stared fear between the eyes and handed the control of that situation over to something unseen.

We all have experienced it again and again. How many times during your college years has the book money run out, your loans maxed out, and you couldn't call home because you felt you would be a burden? And yet you made it through! Have you ever wondered where your next meal would come from and, at the 11th hour, someone stopped by your apartment or dorm room and ordered pizza? Remember, I once lived in a college dormitory that the other students called Hungry Hall. It didn't serve food, but my roommate never sweat it, and neither did I. We got by even though there were days when all we had was peanut butter, crackers and—do I need to repeat it again? Faith. Faith. And more faith.

- **Faith** is what inspired a little Black girl with polio to run track and try out for the Olympics. That girl, Wilma Rudolph, was a sickly child who had to wear a brace on her left leg. Through physical therapy and sheer determination, she conquered her disability and, in 1960, became a champion runner, the first American woman to win three gold medals at a single Olympics.

- **Faith** is what convinced a young dreamer in the inner-city of Dallas that he could hoop even though his height had peaked at five-foot-seven. Relying on speed and remarkable jumping ability, Anthony Jerome "Spud" Webb proved to his detractors that stature has nothing to do with skill. He played with the National Basketball Association (NBA) and was noted for winning a slam dunk contest despite being one of the shortest players in NBA history.

- **Faith** is what drove a young lady from a family of 12 to become owner of a restaurant that paid her to flip burgers as a teen. Her name is Deborah Virgiles and she was one spunky, hard-working girl. When I met her, she was a 16-year-old student at Chadsey High School in Detroit. I hired her to work at my first McDonald's and watched in awe as she rose through the ranks. By the time I had acquired seven franchises, she had moved from the kitchen to the head of my Human Resources department. She was also ready to open her own franchises. Her first two flopped; one in a mall and another in a grocery store. But, propelled by faith, she forged ahead and eventually ended up with several thriving McDonald's restaurants. Deborah, who I am proud to call my mentee, became an American success story—from part-time job to owner. That is the American Dream, is it not?

And is it not the essence of faith? I can say for a fact, that Deborah radiated faith, though I can't claim to know where it comes from. Like Deborah, I feel it in every fiber of my being. But I'm not sure why some people have it and others don't. I have to assume that, for me, it's the result of attending a one-room church in Georgia, built and owned by my family. If you were a child back in my day, faith was instilled in you by elders who made you wash behind your ears and put on your Sunday-go-to-meeting clothes once a week.

All morning and much of the afternoon was spent in a pint-sized building filled with music, stomping, preaching, and joyous celebration. Mind you, if my parents had given me a choice, this would not have been the first thing on my to-do list. But I was accustomed to it and found some aspects pretty cool. Most Sundays, the men of the church handled the preaching and the women served on the usher board. But one Sunday a month was special because the traveling preacher would show up and deliver a fiery sermon. I still remember the big breakfasts of fried chicken, fish, biscuits, bacon, eggs, and gravy that my grandmother, Mammie Gordon, cooked on those days.

Then we'd all gather and pray. I now realize our prayers of "Lord, thank you for waking me up this morning" were creating the foundation for the gratitude and basic decency I live by today. I regard that foundation as my blueprint—not just for support during a crisis or as a means to acquire wealth, but as a way of thinking and being. When you open a franchise with three people and have little or no training, you've got to walk by something other than the McDonald's proven methodology. You need a philosophy on coping, giving, and treating people fairly.

Everyone has to figure out for himself and herself where they want to fit on the faith continuum. But I don't believe I would be where I am today if I had not been taught to adhere to these basic spiritual rules. Faith has sustained me. It has propped me up. When doors were closed, it pointed me toward windows. It has given me a sound moral compass that helped me adhere to the ideals that Morehouse student, Otis Moss, planted within me so many years ago.

I sincerely believe that I have to treat people the way I want to be treated regardless of race, gender, and station in life. I learned, at an early age, to "do unto others as I would have others do unto me." In business, this can be accomplished at the level of management as fair hiring practices and deals that are carried out with integrity.

Or it can be practiced in very basic ways.

I remember one time an elderly man came into one of our McDonald's franchises and ordered a Filet-O-Fish sandwich with mustard. Instead, he was told it would be served with tartar sauce. At the time, that was one of McDonald's standard policies. He complained, but the young lady waiting on him refused to bend. After witnessing this interaction, I had an immediate flashback to the fish fries held at our church in LaGrange every Friday night. I remember vividly that we always slathered yellow mustard on the fish. So this particular evening I bent the rules a bit. Although my employee was following corporate guidelines, I didn't think we had the right to argue with a customer about what he should eat on *his* sandwich.

She kept saying no and brotherman, who no doubt was from the South, kept demanding mustard. Without saying a word, I stepped behind the counter, got a courtesy cup, filled it with mustard and handed it to the gentleman. This was plain, old-fashioned common sense and an example of meeting people where they are. In business, as in life, treat people the way they want to be treated.

I didn't know a thing about karma back then and I don't know much about it now. But I was taught that you reap what you sow, and it's something I will never stop believing. I don't know about most people, but I probably lean a little too much toward my original training. Since I began my career path as a social worker that has stuck with me. I believe in blessing others. I also subscribe to a train of thought shared by activist Marian Wright Edelman: "Service is the rent we pay for being. It is the very purpose of life and not something you do in your spare time."

One day when I was much younger, I started worrying that I had not lived up to that ideal. It seemed to me that, perhaps, I could have done more as a social worker than an entrepreneur. Philanthropist and billionaire Richard DeVos, co-founder of Amway, is the one who turned on the light and woke me up. I was 30 and he was around 50 and I told him how I felt. His answer was priceless.

"Wait a minute," he said. "How many people do you employ?"

"About 70 or 75," I said.

"Well, that's the best social work in the world. You're providing jobs."

I had never thought about it like that. Yet, I have no doubt in my mind that without my spiritual focus, I would have kept more money to myself and not be as fulfilled as I am today. Everyone has to decide for herself and himself how they want to give back or pay it forward. For some, it might be organizing a scuba diver club. Obviously, that's not Bill Pickard. For others, it might be mentoring a young man in math or calculus or teaching Sunday School.

There are various ways we can all serve. Some people donate time, some people write a check, some can do both. Be grateful you have the capacity to do either. No matter how successful you become, never forget to be supremely thankful for your blessings and remember "to whom much is given, much is required." You have a responsibility to assist those who are less fortunate. As a man of faith, I see it as an obligation.

Not everyone agrees with me, but I also have the idealistic notion that pathology can be turned into "hopeology." That's a term I coined to explain that lives can be transformed by scholarships, job training, and counseling. I've heard stories of at-risk youth whose attitudes did an about-face after meeting the right person, being exposed to an uplifting program, or landing a good opportunity.

So my parting advice is that you keep ascending the ladder and when you get to the top, reach back. Pathology dwells on the urban malaise of broken families, students performing below their grade level, the cradle-to-grave prison pipeline. But the social worker who still resides in me doesn't feel the need to paint the entire predicament with one broad brush stroke. Young men and women with yearnings, talent, and potential can be found everywhere, and genius can emerge from the worst conditions.

I suppose this is the real reason I became an entrepreneur. The old joke is that an entrepreneur is someone who will work 80 hours a week for himself to avoid working 40 hours a week for someone else. Maybe. But we also do it because we know that, one day, we will be in the position to pass on all that we have gained—and learned.

This is what I am doing now with this book. I've rounded up all of my experiences and humbly placed them in your lap. What are you going to do with them? Will you shrug and say you're tired of people trying to give you directions? Or will you step out like I did? On faith. The principle of faith is the culmination of all seven of my entrepreneurship principles. The **vision and attitude** you hold in your heart, the **opportunities** you seize, the **finances** you secure, the **relationships** you cultivate, the **talent** you hire, and the **failure** you transcend are all the result of your **faith**. Faith is the golden key and with it, everything else will lock itself into place.

Good luck! And remember: Rivers get choppy and highways aren't always smooth, but no matter what stressors you encounter —high taxes, credit issues, defaulted loans —never lose sight of one fact: The banker you're dealing with might be a hell of a banker, but the God you serve is the CEO.

APPENDIX

The Next Step and Where to Learn More

PRINCIPLE ONE · VISION

Steps to Action

Vision Boards—Vision Boards are the visualization of what you want to achieve. They were popularized in the book, *The Secret*. Novellus Financial (2014), states, "Love it or hate it, vision boards are an entrepreneur's best friend."

Vision boards should focus on big dreams, what you want to achieve, what you want to feel. They should help you bring your vision to life. This is known as the "The Law of Attraction." You are depicting what you want to "attract" to your life.

Mark Twain once said, "You can't depend on your eyes when your imagination is out of focus."

Vision boards are a form of visual inspiration. They should be displayed in a place where they can be viewed on a regular basis. They can also be regarded as a form of a visual business plan. One way to do this is to share your vision with your consumers on a site such as Pinterest. As always, be careful what you share since it is all public.

Types of Vision Boards

Goal Orientation, Philosophy Orientation, Performance Orientation (Bet-David, 2016)

What You Need:

- A Board – Styrofoam, Cork Board, Poster Board (Need to determine the proper size)

- Markers, Colors, Glue, Glue Gun, Sparkles, Thumb Tacks

- Magazines, Printed Pictures from the Internet Scissors, Paint, Stickers

- Quotes, Photos, Time (Rider, 2015; Scott, 2014; Scully, 2011)

What to Do:

Acknowledge what are you grateful for. Acknowledge what you want to achieve. Acknowledge what you have achieved. Acknowledge "The Law of Attraction." Look at your board regularly daily. (Canfield, 2014)

Where to Learn More:

Susannah Scully. (2011). How to make a vision board. (YouTube)
www.youtube.com/watch?v=IVkxoHou-BU

Nik Scott. (2014). How to create a vision board & make it work. (YouTube)
www.youtube.com/watch?v=4G-T2uLgOIQ

PRINCIPLE TWO — OPPORTUNITY

Steps to Action

To find opportunities or to have them find you, think about the following:

- Finding your niche. What are you good at?

- Becoming a guru. Always be continually improving and moving forward. Knowledge is power.

- Giving to receive. The Golden Rule: In everything, do to others as you would have them do to you. Matthew 7:12

- Having filters. Not every idea is a "good" idea.

- Putting optimism aside.

- Assessing realistic requirements. If you cannot complete this task, then you will not understand the financials, and the business plan cannot be developed.

- Committing with limits. Know when things are "not" working.

- Be challenged.

- Be aware. Stay in "tune" with the environment around you. Understand what is going on in your industry and community.

- Be fearless. Things do not get done unless you implement. Implementation means it is time to put the "fear" to the side.

- Be decisive.

- Make an impact. Touch someone's life, an industry, or a community with the service or a product you provide. Whose life will you make better?

- Imagine all opportunities.

- Jump into hot markets. Can you take advantage of a trend? Can you make the "hot" product better?

- Listen. How can your vendors/suppliers help you be better? What do your customers want?

- What do you want?

- Imitate and improve. There is no reason to "reinvent the wheel." Make it roll better.

- Simplify.

- Align Strengths with Opportunities.

- Shore Up Weaknesses. (Banjeree, 2013; "Capitalizing on Business," n.d.; Christie, 2016; Daum, n.d.; Pressley, 2014; Seifert, n.d.

Where to Learn More

Sanjeev Bikhchandani. (2015, November). How to identify a business opportunity. (TEDx on YouTube) www.youtube.com/watch?v=OkN-psVMT84w

Karen Anderson. (2014, September). Be an opportunity maker. (TEDx on YouTube) www.ted.com/talks/kare_anderson_be_an_opportunity_maker

PRINCIPLE THREE – FINANCE

Steps to Action

The keys to investing and building wealth include:

- Recognizing that wealth takes time to build. One does not invest for the short term.

- One needs to work hard every day. This includes learning new skills which make you more valuable and allows you to save more.

- Be consistent. Again, nothing happens overnight.

- You don't have to keep up with the "Joneses," and don't spend all the new income.

- Build your wealth with assets that appreciate. One does not need the fastest or newest car or the largest apartment or house. Most millionaires have been the same house for 20 years (Brokamp, 2016).

- Be debt free.

- Pay your credit cards in full every month.

- Direct Deposit into your savings account, your individual retirement account, your 401(k), or your 403(b). What you don't see, you cannot spend.

- Get a second job. It builds your wealth and keeps you too busy to spend the money.

- Find a job you like. You don't have to do something you don't like to build wealth.

- Have a plan. Have a vision. Set big goals. When asked "Do you know how much your family spends each year on food, clothing, and shelter?" you need to be able to answer "yes." Almost two-thirds of millionaires can say "yes," while 35% of high-income non-millionaires say "no." (Brokamp, 2016).

• Have insurance.

Where to Learn More:

Steve Harvey. (2013, March 12). Steve Harvey "Get Your Hustle On" Live from DDA 2013 [Disney Dreamers Academy]. (YouTube) www.youtube.com/watch?v=I846NzfR3hU

Steve Harvey. (2015, August 6). Steve Harvey Uncut: If you quit, you'll never know. (YouTube) https://youtu.be/bu0GTy1ZTnI

Margaret Hefferman. (2015, May). Forget the pecking order at work. (TED www.ted.com/talks/margaret_heffernan_why_it_s_time_to_forget_the_pecking_order at_work

Ben Lumley. (2015, Mary 29). Hustle and grind. (TED) tedxtalks.ted.com/video/Hustle-and-Grind-Ben-Lumley-TED;search%3Ahustle

APPENDIX

PRINCIPLE FOUR – RELATIONSHIPS

Steps to Action

To take the discomfort out of networking (in person or online):

- Don't talk about work. You are trying to meet people. Talk to them about "them." Again, it is not all about you and what they can do for you. Or, at least that is the way it should be approached.

- Have a support system. Take a friend to a networking event. But, don't clutch on to the acquaintance. Move out and about.

- Ask questions. Have a series of ice breaking questions. This method also reduces other's perceptions of you being aggressive if you are only talking about yourself. However, be willing to open up. Otherwise, the other party may feel it is an interrogation.

- Have an elevator pitch ready. This way you can explain your business quickly and move on. If they really want to know more, they will ask. This shows you are prepared to "sell" yourself if the opportunity is provided.

- Meet a variety of individuals. One never knows when that new acquaintance can be of help in the future. It is not all about meeting the "big cheese" in the room. However, one must also be intentional in who you meet and the relationships you want to build.

- Join conversations. "Read" the group to determine if you are actually welcomed to the conversation.

- Don't monopolize the conversation. Listening is just as important.

- Names are important. Try to remember them, repeat the name, get a business card, and ask again when in doubt.

- Follow up with your new acquaintances. Don't say you will follow up with someone and then fail to do so.

- For the introverted, make sure you make an effort to stay at least 20 minutes. It provides a goal and if things are going smoothly then the time frame can be extended.

- Practice, practice, practice. The more you network at work, social events, and actual networking events, the easier it becomes. Make it fun.

- Volunteer – Chamber of Commerce, charities, local university events, alumni events for your alma mater, etc.

- Take notes. So you remember the conversation, take notes on the business card you may have received. If there is not a card, that is what the note taking app on your phone is for.

- Don't spam. People don't want spam in their e-mails and they don't want spam in their wallets. Don't blindly pass out business cards. Let them ask or "feel out" the situation before offering your card to the other party.

- Have a professional e-mail. This is especially important for students or recent graduates. If possible, you should create your own website and tie it to your e-mail.

- Keep your e-mail signature professional. No emoticons and use basic Arial or Times New Roman in a 10 or 12 font. Think normal!

- Make sure you have a clean online reputation. In today's environment, you will be Googled. Be polished.

  - Your LinkedIn information needs to be up-to-date.
  - Your Facebook presence needs to be active and clean. You have to consider reducing your number of friends. Be careful of the kinds of pictures that are taken of you at events and when you are being tagged.
  - Your Instagram, Snapchat, Vine, and Pinterest pages are also subject to review.
  - Blog and Tweet. These avenues allow you to expand your visibility. Just make sure you are providing information that is necessary and effective.

- Follow industry leaders on Twitter or LinkedIn.(Brustein, 2015; D'Antonio & Iannucci, 2014)

Where to Learn More

Dan Nechita. (2016, May 11). Networking is a form of education. (TED)tedxtalks.ted.com/video/Networking-is-a-form-of-educati;-search%3Adan%20nechita

Sheryl Sandberg. (2010, December). Why we have too few women leaders. (TED) www.ted.com/talks/sheryl_sandberg_why_we_have_too_few_ women_leaders

PRINCIPLE FIVE – TALENT AND SKILLSET

Steps to Action

Having the right people around you is a MUST. They can be advisors, doers, or experts. Consider the following when hiring those to work with you or under you:

- The mission must feel right. Employees need to identify with the mission and be committed.

- Information must flow freely. Employees cannot be left in the "dark" if you expect them to act like owners.

- People must feel valued. Employees must be engaged in their work. It is important that employees know their part in the organization's decision making. This defines the organization's "power distance." This would encourage leadership not to micromanage.

- People must feel powerful. Employees must have control over their work. This also means the bureaucratic structure is reduced. It means that everyone is accountable for performance standards and for values being upheld. This is also important to scaling the culture as the company grows.

- One should lead by example, not by announcement. Organizational leaders need to lead by wandering around. Be "out and about" with your employees. Leaders must be transparent with their employees.

- Equity should prevail. Be consistent. Individuals should be treated fairly in promotion and perks. Favoritism is not relevant. Don't discriminate. Everyone has a right to their opinion.

- Coach everyone. Transfer knowledge. Develop your employees' skills.

- Embrace new ideas from new employees. Otherwise, there will be too much "inbreeding" and a stagnant culture will be created. (Bouton, 2015; Brown & Gutterman, 2012; Conte, 2014; deSilva, 2013; Edmonds, 2012; Google Ventures, 2012; Miller, 2014; Rockwell, 2014; Schwartz, 2014; Watkins, 2013; Wilkinson, 2012.)

Where to Learn More

Yvonne Conte. (2014, October 13). Corporate culture that works. (TED)tedxtalks.ted.com/video/Corporate-culture-that-works-%7C;-search%3AY vonne%20Conte

Google Ventures. (2012, December 20). Foundation: Tony Hsieh On building a great company culture. (YouTube) from www.youtube.com/watch?v =VZHr4JOl1LM

Barry Schwartz. (2014, March). The way we think about work is broken. (TED) www.ted.com/talks/barry_schwartz_the_way_we_think_about_work_is_broken

Jay Wilkinson. (2012, August 24). Company culture. (TED) tedxtalks.ted.com/video/TEDxLincoln-Jay-Wilkinson-Compa;search%3 AJay%20Wilkinson

PRINCIPLE SIX – FAILURE

Steps to Action

What should you learn from failure to become successful? Consider the following:

- Confront fear and learn from it. However, realize you cannot control everything. On the other hand, don't let a loss define you. Have courage!

- Be responsible. This is not time to pass the proverbial "buck" and play the "blame game." It is a time to learn. It means to be reflective.

- Build your own team. Don't depend on what others have done in the past. It may not fit your style and it may cause you failure. Be proactive. This also means you should realize your limitations and understand what "you don't know." Find the right advisors or employees.

- Trust your gut. For those straight out of high school or college, you still have some wisdom to collect, but ask the right questions and go with your instincts.

- Take your second chance. Remember, failure is a chance to find the next opportunity. After all, 8 out of 10 businesses fail. On the other hand, don't let the statistic create unnecessary fear in your first venture.

- Appreciate your responsibilities to others (customers, employees, family, or friends). If you fail, then others may be affected. Pay attention to your daily and weekly plan. If you do fail, explain why it will not happen a second time.

- Don't keep accelerating a bad idea. Step back and reevaluate.

- Be a realist. As Saltzman (2014) stated, "true hustlers grind through it." Also, the next project may not be right around the corner. As Andew Yang, CEO of Venture for America told Parmar (2014), "Bouncing back takes time and is a 'gradual' process."

- Learn lean. Corroborate assumptions before moving forward on projects. Treat failure like a scientist. It is simply another data point.

- Be reflective. Understand why things may have gone wrong. (Clear, 2014; Demers, 2014)

Answer the following questions:

- What is failure?
- Have you failed?
- Is failure useful? Have you learned from your failure?
- How have you reacted, if ever, to failure?
- Have you been failed by friends, family, co-workers, etc?
- If you answered "yes," how did you react?"
- In examining your home, work, school or organizations, do you see failure?
- If "yes," can it be fixed? (Slotnik & Schulten, 2012)

Where to Learn More

Astro Teller. (2016, February). The unexpected benefit of celebrating failure. (TED) www.ted.com/talks/astro_teller_the_unexpected_benefit_of_celebrating_failure

Sarah Lewis. (2014, March). Embrace the near win. (TED) www.ted.com/talks/sarah_lewis_embrace_the_near_win

Eddie Obeng. (2012, June). Smart failure for a fast-changing world. (TED) www.ted.com/talks/eddie_obeng_smart_failure_for_a_fast_changing_world

Kathryn Schulz. (2011, March). On being wrong. (TED)tedxtalks.ted.com/video/Servant-Leadership-%7C-Joe-Schmit;search% 3Aservant%20leadership

Tom Wujec. (2010, February). Build a tower, build a team. (TED) marshmallow challenge.com/Instructions_files/TED2010_Tom_Wujec_Marshmallow_Challenge_Web_Version.pdf

PRINCIPLE SEVEN – FAITH

Steps to Action

Traits of servant leaders for consideration:

- An ability to shift between thoughts, circumstances and events quickly. They do so without losing focus.

- Confidence in their abilities. They are able to ignore the critics when needed. They are able to overcome self-doubt.

- An understanding of the value of self talk. As Krakowski (2014) noted, "Our bottom line and our daily output are completely dependent on our self talk." What do we say and what do we not say. What if someone could read our daily thoughts? As with ignoring the critics when needed, we need to believe in ourselves.

- Vision. As Baugus (2013) notes, "Profitable entrepreneurship requires both vision and faith. The entrepreneurial process begins when a person has the vision for a better world and the faith that he can bring that about."

- Sacrifice and service. This refers to the concept of servant leadership.

- Perseverance. Refer to the economic concept of "creative destruction" developed by Joseph Schumpeter. Leaders and business concepts must both overcome obstacles. People have to have the right self talk. Business needs the right product or service and then work to constantly improve it; in essence, destroying the previous product for the new one's birth. (Baugus, 2013; Daum, 2103; Economy, 2015; Hennessey, 2013; Krakowski, 2014)

Follow the steps above closely. Also rely on the following spiritual practices:

1. Be Thankful—Express gratitude for the blessings, opportunities and joys that fill you with appreciation – wonders of the world, family, health, etc.

2. Be Humble—Acknowledge those who help you.

3. Be Hopeful—Acknowledge what you are asking to receive.

4. Be Open—Be willing to accept what you are receiving and make the most of it.

Where to Learn More

Chris Hintz. (2012, December 18). Servant leadership. (TED) tedxtalks. ted.com/video/Servant-Leadership-Chris-Hintz;search%3Aservant%20 leadership

David Michael. (2016, May 21).

Riding the right wave. (TED) tedxtalks.ted.com/video/Riding-the-Right-Wave-David-Mic;search%3Adavid%20michael

Conor Neill. (2013, November 26). Entrepreneurial leadership: Faith, hope, & love. (YouTube) www.youtube.com/watch?v=06xkQAaFZJs

Joe Schmitt. (2014, December 3). Servant leadership. (TED[x]) tedxtalks. ted.com/video/Servant-Leadership-%7C-Joe-Schmit;search%3Aservant%20leadership University of the Southwest (USW) Mustangs. (2013, February 20). Servant Leadership. (YouTube) https:/www.youtube.com/watch?v=XlTzLd6oXC0

The Next Step and Where to Learn More was compiled by Janel Bell-Haynes, Ph.D. and Sara Kiser, Ph.D. Dr. Haynes is professor of marketing and chair of the business administration department at Alabama State University. Dr. Kiser is professor of management at Alabama State University and serves on the editorial board for the Society for the Advancement of Management.

REFERENCES

Banerjee, J. (2013, December 23). *Billionaire vision: How to capitalize on opportunity.* Retrieved June 28, 2016, from www.jeetbanerjee.com/how-to-capitalize-on-opportunity/

Baugus, B. (2013, June 19). Five Christian traits every entrepreneur needs. Retrieved July 2, 2016, from tifwe.org/five-christian-traits-every-entrepreneur-needs/

Bet-David, P. (2016, March 15). Three types of vision boards for entrepreneurs. Retrieved July 1, 2016, from www.patrickbetdavid.com/3-types-vision-boards-entrepreneurs/ (This includes a 16-minute video).

Bouton, K. (2015, July 17). Recruiting cultural fit. *Harvard Business Review.* Retrieved July 30, 2015, from hbr.org/2015/07/recruiting-for-cultural-fit

Brokamp, R. (2016, May 2). Nine lessons in wealth-building from the millionaire next door. Retrieved July 3, 2016, from www.getrichslowly.org/blog/2011/02/09/nine-lessons-in-wealth-building-from-the-millionaire-next-door/

Brown, R., & Gutterman, A. S. (2012, December 13). Questions to guide you in understanding your organizational culture. Retrieved December 14, 2012, from www.smartbrief.com/original/2012/12/questions-guide-you-understanding-your-organizational-culture

Brustein, D. (2014, July 22). *17 tips to survive your next networking event.* Retrieved November 10, 2015 from www.forbes.com/sites/yec/2014/07/22/17-tips-to-survive-your-next-networking-event/

Canfield, J. (2014, December 3). How to create an empowering vision board. Retrieved June 28, 2016, jackcanfield.com/how-to-create-an-empowering-vision-book/#

Capitalizing on business opportunities. (n.d.) Retrieved June 29, 2016, from business-knowledgesource.com /blog/capitalizing_on_businessopportunities_032307.html

Christie, I. (n.d.). *Create your own opportunities.* Retrieved June 29, 2016, from www.monster.com/career-advice/article/Create-Opportunities

Clear, J. (2014, March 10). Afraid of failure? Think like a scientist and get over it. *Entrepreneur*. Retrieved September 10, 2014, from www.entrepreneur.com/article/232024

D'Antonio, J., & Iannucci, M. (2014, January 31). 5 big tips for connecting with young professionals. Retrieved November 10, 2015 from www.bizjournals.com/philadelphia/blog/guest-comment/2014/01/5-big-tips-for-connecting-with-young.html

Daum, K. (n.d.). Make the most of any opportunity. *Inc*. Retrieved June 29, 2016, from www.inc.com/kevin-daum/make-the-most-of-any-opportunity.html

deSilva, J. (2103, June 4). *Ryan Estis, on company culture and how to do it right*. Retrieved June 5, 2013, from www.smartbrief.com/original/2013/06/ryan-estis-company-culture-and-how-do-it-right

Demers, J. (2014, July). Successful entrepreneurs thrive in failure, so embrace it when it's inevitable. *Entrepreneur*. Retrieved September 10, 2014, from www.entrepreneur.com/article/235760

Edmonds, S. C. (2012, November 20). *Corporate culture changes only when people change*. Retrieved December 14, 2012 from www.smartbrief.com/original/2012/11/corporate-culture-changes-only-when-people-change

Economy, P. (2105, January 26). 7 secrets of 'servant leadership' that will lead you to success. Retrieved July 2, 2016, from www.inc.com/peter-economy/7-secrets-of-servant-leadership-that-will-lead-you-to-success.html

Hennessey, R. (2013, November 27). What role should religious values play in business? *Entrepreneur*. Retrieved July 2, 2016, from www.entrepreneur.com/article/230145

Krawkowski, S. (2014, February 12). The winning traits of faith based leaders. *Inc*. Retrieved July 2, 2016, from www.entrepreneur.com/article/231425

Miller, J. (2014, June 2). *How to foster a coaching culture in your company*. Retrieved June 6, 2014, from people-equation.com/how-to-foster-a-coaching-culture-in-your-company/

Novellus Financial (2014, November 21). Why are vision boards a necessity for entrepreneurs? Retrieved July 1, 2016, from novellusfinancialnews.com/vision-boards-necessity-entrepreneurs/

Parmar, N. (2014, April 22). Failure: Going from moping to hoping. *Entrepreneur*. Retrieved September 10, 2014, from www.entrepreneur.com/article/232963

Pressley, D. (2014, September 12). *Take advantage of workplace opportunities to enhance your career*. Retrieved June 29, 2016, from www.theworkathomewoman.com/taking-advantage-of-opportunities/

Rider, E. (2015, January 12). The reason vision boards work and how to make one. *Huffington Post*. Retrieved June 28, 2016, from www.youtube.com/watch?v=IVkx-oHou-BU

Rockwell, D. (2014, July 21). *10 ways to create a sense of ownership*. Retrieved 9, 2014, from leadershipfreak.wordpress.com/2014/07/21/10-ways-to-create-a-sense-of-ownership/

Saltzman, J. (2014, June 23). 6 tips for accepting failure and moving on. *Entrepreneur*. Retrieved September 10, 2014, from www.entrepreneur.com/article/235078

Seifert, B. (n.d.). *Taking advantage of opportunities in front of you*. Retrieved from www.theworkathomewoman.com/taking-advantage-of-opportunities/

Slotnik, D. E., & Schulten, K. (2012, May 17). *How to help students understand the lessons of failure*. Retrieved July 4, 2016, from www.howtolearn.com/2012/05/how-to-help-students-understand-the-lessons-of-failure/

Watkins, M. (2013, May 15). What is organizational culture? And why should we care? *Harvard Business Review*. Retrieved January 2, 2014, from hbr.org/2013/05/what-is-organizational-culture/

ABOUT THE AUTHOR

William F. Pickard launched his entrepreneurial journey as a McDonald's franchisee in Detroit, Michigan, more than three decades ago. In 1989, he founded an automotive manufacturing company and grew it into the Global Automotive Alliance, a network of logistics and manufacturing firms with more than a half billion dollars in sales and eight plants in the United States and Canada. He is chairman of GAA, co-managing partner of MGM Grand Detroit Casino, CEO of Bearwood Management Company and co-owner of five Black-owned newspapers.

A life member of Alpha Phi Alpha fraternity, Pickard has served on numerous business and non-profit boards including Asset Acceptance Capital Corporation, Michigan National Bank, LaSalle Bank, Business Leaders for Michigan, National Urban League, Detroit Symphony Orchestra, and the Detroit Black Chamber of Commerce. In 2001, he was awarded *Michiganian of the Year* for his business success, civic leadership and philanthropy. He was the first chairman of the African Development Foundation in 1982, appointed by President Ronald Reagan. Under President George Bush, he was appointed to the National Advisory Committee on Trade Policy Negotiations in 1990 and the Federal Home Loan Bank Board-Indianapolis Bank in Indiana in 1991.

He holds a bachelor's degree from Western Michigan University, a master's degree from the University of Michigan, and a Ph.D. from The Ohio State University.

ABOUT THE WRITER

Denise Crittendon was the founding editor of the former *African American Family Magazine* in Metro Detroit and the first woman in the history of the NAACP to be appointed editor of its national magazine, *The Crisis*. A former features writer for the *Kansas City Star*, she also spent 15 years as a reporter and features writer for *The Detroit News*. Ms. Crittendon is the recipient of a magazine writing award from the National Association of Black Journalists and column writing awards from Parenting Publications of America and the Detroit Chapter of the Society of Professional Journalists. She is the author of *Girl In The Mirror: A Teen's Guide To Self Awareness*.